AMERICANS
THE *Spirit* OF A *Nation*

MATHEW BRADY

"The Camera Is the Eye of History"

Don Nardo

Enslow Publishers, Inc.
40 Industrial Road
Box 398
Berkeley Heights, NJ 07922
USA

http://www.enslow.com

Library of Congress Cataloging-in-Publication Data:

Nardo, Don, 1947–
    Mathew Brady : "the camera is the eye of history" / Don Nardo.
      p. cm. — (Americans—the spirit of a nation)
    Includes bibliographical references and index.
      Summary: "Examines the life of photographer Mathew Brady, the advancements he made in photography, his work during the Civil War, and his legacy as the first great photographer in American History"—Provided by publisher.
    ISBN-13: 978-0-7660-3023-7
    ISBN-10: 0-7660-3023-7
      1. Brady, Mathew B., 1823 (ca.)–1896—Juvenile literature. 2. Photographers—United States—Biography—Juvenile literature. I. Title.
    TR140.B7N37 2008
    770.92—dc22
    [B]
                                        2007044886

Printed in the United States of America

10 9 8 7 6 5 4 3 2 1

To Our Readers:
We have done our best to make sure all Internet Addresses in this book were active and appropriate when we went to press. However, the author and the publisher have no control over and assume no liability for the material available on those Internet sites or on other Web sites they may link to. Any comments or suggestions can be sent by e-mail to comments@enslow.com or to the address on the back cover.

☘ Enslow Publishers, Inc., is committed to printing our books on recycled paper. The paper in every book contains 10% to 30% post-consumer waste (PCW). The cover board on the outside of each book contains 100% PCW. Our goal is to do our part to help young people and the environment too!

CONTENTS

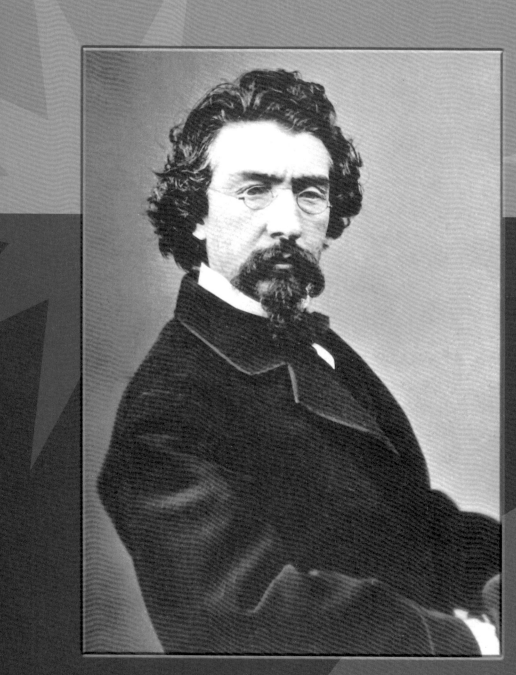

Mathew Brady

Chapter

1

War Is No Picnic

Thirty-eight-year-old photographer Mathew Brady followed a column of U.S. troops. They were marching southward from Washington, D.C., the country's capital. A few months before, in April 1861, the American Civil War had begun. The North, or Union, was pitted against the South, or Confederacy. They were about to clash in the war's first battle, at Bull Run, a shallow waterway some thirty miles southwest of Washington.

Brady was accompanied by a sketch artist and two newspaper reporters. They were not the only civilians present. Thousands of people of all walks of life traveled behind the soldiers. There were reporters, congressmen, and many other civilians, including women and children.[1] They were sure the Union troops would quickly defeat their opponents. The volleys of gunfire would make for an entertaining show. And then, with the war over in a single battle, everyone would go home.

But when the fighting began on July 21, 1861, many Union soldiers were badly wounded. In horror, the onlookers watched these men bleeding and dying. Horses twitched in their death agonies. And it swiftly became clear to all that the war would be no picnic.

The Crush of Human Flesh

For a while, the frightened and wounded Union recruits managed to hold their ground. It is not known for sure what Brady did during these fateful hours. No evidence has survived to show that he actually managed to take any pictures. This may have been because the battle was so chaotic and dangerous. A reporter for the *New York Tribune*, William A. Croffut, later wrote about meeting Brady that day. "I asked him if he could get the fellows who were fighting to stand still and look pleasant," Croffut recalled:

> *With a very serious face, he said he supposed not. But he could probably get some [photos of] scenes that would be worthwhile. . . . On his back was a camera. . . . I saw him afterwards dodging shells on the battlefield. He was in motion but his machine did not seem effective. And when about two o'clock a runaway team of horses came dashing wildly past us . . . I saw Brady again and shouted, "Now's your time [to take some photos]!" But I failed to stir him. I have often wondered how many pictures he took that day.*[2]

Brady was certainly unable to take any photos during the Union retreat that suddenly ensued. A little past 4:00 P.M., the Confederates launched a headlong charge. In the words of one historian, "A strange, eerie scream rent the air." It was the Confederates' battle cry. "Soon to be known as the rebel yell, this unearthly wail struck fear into the hearts of the enemy."[3] Indeed, most of the Union soldiers panicked. Brady surely heard the scary battle cry, too. And he and his wagons were soon in the midst of fleeing men and horses. One of the congressmen at the scene later described these frightened troops who surrounded Brady: "A cruel, crazy, mad hopeless panic possessed them. . . . Their mouths gaped, their lips [were] cracked and blackened with [gun]powder . . . their eyes [stared] in frenzy. No mortal ever saw such a mass of ghastly wretches."[4]

"Our apparatus was a good deal damaged on the way back to Washington."

The civilians saw the human tide approaching. Terrified, these men, women, and children dropped whatever they were carrying and ran screaming toward Washington. Soon the crush of human and animal flesh smashed into Brady's wagons. And one of them overturned. "Our apparatus was a good deal damaged on the way back to Washington," Brady later said.[5]

A Sense of Destiny

At the time of First Bull Run, Brady was one of the best-known photographers in the United States. His studios

7

First Bull Run and the Great Skedaddle

Mathew Brady attempted to photograph the first major land battle of the American Civil War. It is most often called First Bull Run. This is to tell it apart from another battle fought in the same place later in the war. First Bull Run is also referred to as the First Battle of Manassas.

More than sixty thousand troops eventually converged at Bull Run. About half represented the Union. The other half were Confederates. For a while, the Union soldiers were able to make headway. They pushed a number of Confederate units back.

But then a large group of Union troops encountered an entrenched unit led by Confederate Brigadier General Thomas J. Jackson. Jackson's men opened fire with devastating effect. Many Union soldiers fell dead instantly. The rest panicked and fled. Their headlong retreat came to be called the "Great Skedaddle." When the guns finally fell silent, Union casualties were about 2,650, including 418 dead. The Confederates had about 1,980 casualties, among them 387 killed.[6]

in New York and Washington, D.C., were always busy. Usually, he created posed portraits for his customers. They either stood or sat in a chair. And they made sure to hold as still as possible for several seconds. Cameras were still in their technical infancy. And the crude photographic plates they used required long exposures.

It was unusual for Brady to take his equipment outside his studio. But the outbreak of war seemed to warrant it. Hearing that a great battle was about to take place at Bull Run, Brady had scrambled to prepare. He recognized the enormous potential of photography. It could be used for much more than creating still portraits, he realized. Photos capturing battles and other major events could be sold by the thousands. A skilled and ambitious photographer could make a great deal of money.

Brady also realized that such photos could become valuable historical records. And he and his work might be remembered and treasured by future generations. Taking photos in the field would be dangerous, he knew. He might be shot or captured by the enemy. But a sense of destiny overcame his fears. "I felt I had to go," he later recalled. "A spirit in my feet said *go*, and I went!"[7]

Brady quickly came to see that working in the field would be difficult as well as dangerous. First, his cameras were large and much too heavy for a person to carry long distances. Also, he would need a portable darkroom. Horse-drawn wagons had seemed to be the most practical solution to these problems. Brady had loaded his cameras and food into one wagon. The other wagon had become his darkroom.

During the Civil War, Brady used wagons to carry his equipment and as darkrooms to develop his photos.

As Brady had followed the Union troops toward Bull Run, he had prudently dressed for the weather. It had been sunny and very hot. So he had worn a white, lightweight linen jacket and a white straw hat. These garments reflected sunlight, helping to keep him cool. Meanwhile, the hat's wide brim ensured that his forehead and nose would not get sunburned. A thick mustache and goatee protected the lower portion of his face.

At this point, Brady had no inkling that Bull Run would be a disaster for the North. He did not foresee that soon he would be on this very same road. Only this time he would be running for his life in the opposite direction.

Brady's War Trophy

At some point during his experience at the First Battle of Bull Run, Mathew Brady obtained a sword from a Union soldier. The exact circumstances are unknown. But it is certain that Brady carried the sword back to his studio in Washington.

Only hours after arriving, he had an assistant take a photo of him. It shows him wearing his field outfit—including his white coat and wide-brimmed straw hat. The outline of his new sword is visible beneath his coat.

A Player in History

Brady made it back to Washington in the late afternoon of July 22. The grim news was just as he had feared. The Union had lost the battle, later called First Bull Run. Both northerners and southerners now saw that the war was not going to be easy and swift. It was going to be a long and difficult struggle.

Brady had little or nothing to show for his efforts at Bull Run. He had taken no photos and much of his equipment had been destroyed during the chaotic retreat. It is significant, and somewhat strange, that some people believed that he *had* produced photos of the battle. *Humphrey's Journal of Photography* reported on August 15, 1861, that Brady "has been in Virginia with his camera, and many and spirited are the pictures he has taken." The journal added, "His are the only reliable records of the fight at Bull's Run." Also, "The groups of entire regiments and divisions, within a space of a couple of feet square, present some of the most curious effects as yet produced in photography."[8]

Yet no such photos of the First Bull Run battle have ever surfaced. As Bob Zeller, a noted expert on Civil War photography, points out:

A listing of "Brady's Photographic Views of the War" in the November 1862 edition of the Anthony Company's catalog of card photographs describes more than 300 war photographs. But not one is identified as having been taken during the campaign of First Bull Run in 1861. Had

Brady taken any, he would have cataloged and marketed them.[9]

Brady did eventually photograph the Bull Run battlefield. This occurred in March 1862, long after the battle was over. Brady sent his assistants George Bernard and James Gibson to the scene of the conflict. There, they took photos of some Confederate fortifications. They also captured images of the graves of Union soldiers killed in the battle and the ruins of a burned railroad station.

In March 1862, Brady's photographers James Gibson and George Barnard went to Bull Run and took pictures of the First Bull Run's aftermath. This photo shows the ruins of a stone bridge.

These and other photos taken later by Brady or his assistants became important documents of the Civil War. In the years that followed, they took their cameras into many military campaigns. They also recorded images of key places on numerous battlefields, usually after the fighting was over. Brady also took several excellent photos of key figures in the Civil War. Among them were President Abraham Lincoln, Union general Ulysses S. Grant, and Confederate general Robert E. Lee.

In this way, Brady became a major player in history, as well as a key recorder of it. He was not the only active or successful Civil War photographer. But he either employed or inspired most of them. His importance in that regard is well summed up by scholar William A. Frassanito:

> *It cannot be denied that Mathew Brady, perhaps more than any other individual, was the prime mover of initial efforts to establish a corps of photographers who would [thoroughly] cover the war on a grand scale. Without his organizational and leadership abilities, along with his financial backing, it is doubtful that the war would have been covered as extensively as it was.*[10]

A Young Man in the Big City

The early years of the United States's first great photographer are veiled in mystery. In 1891, when he was nearly seventy, Mathew B. Brady agreed to be interviewed. The interviewer asked his age. But Brady could no longer remember his exact birth date. It might have been 1823, he said, or it might have been 1824. (More recent scholarship has suggested it was 1822.)

As for his birthplace, Brady was only slightly more helpful. He came from Warren County, in upstate New York, he told the interviewer. It was

Brady said that he grew up in the area around Lake George in New York State. This painting depicts how the area looked during the time he lived there.

"in the woods around Lake George." However, Brady no longer recalled the exact location of his parents' house. He identified his parents as Andrew and Julia Brady. His father, Andrew, "was an Irishman," Brady added.[1] Mathew Brady may have thought that his parents were born in the United States. This "fact" is listed on his death certificate. But most historians believe Andrew and Julia Brady were born in Ireland. The Bradys most likely came to America in about 1820.

Brady did recall that his parents owned a small farm. As a boy, he performed standard farm chores. That is all he ever revealed about his boyhood. He was always very reluctant to talk about his personal life. He even claimed that his middle initial, "B," stood for nothing.

Brady gave only two major published interviews in his life—one in 1891 and another in 1893. Outside of these, he was almost mute. He wrote no autobiography. Nor did he write a single article about his life. In addition, he did not keep a diary, and he only seldom wrote letters.

As a result, most of what is known about Brady comes from two sets of sources. First, there are a number of administrative documents. These include his appointment books, legal records, and so forth. The second and more important source consists of the recollections of people he knew. Among these are relatives, friends, neighbors, employers, his assistants, and several of the people he photographed. Historians have pieced these scattered sources together. The result is a somewhat vague but fairly reliable picture of Brady's life.

An Aspiring Painter

In 1839, at the age of sixteen, Mathew suffered from "inflammation of the eyes."[2] Today that condition is called conjunctivitis. Among its symptoms are redness around the eyes along with a watery discharge. Hoping for a cure, the young man traveled to neighboring Saratoga Springs. That town was widely known for its natural spring waters. Supposedly these waters had significant health benefits.

While in Saratoga, Mathew met a twenty-eight-year-old artist named William Page. In nearby Albany, Page had a studio where he painted portraits for a living. Mathew and Page quickly became friends, and the older man invited the younger to spend some time in Albany. There, Mathew helped in Page's studio, washing brushes, stretching canvases, and performing other tasks.

Almost immediately, Mathew developed an interest in painting. Page encouraged his friend. He "gave me a bundle of his crayons to copy," Mathew later recalled.[3] (By "crayons," he meant crayon drawings.) In this way, Mathew learned to draw. Page also showed him the basics of oil painting.

Early Pioneers of Photography

Only a few months later, Page decided to leave Albany for New York. Mathew agreed to go with him. The exact reason for the move is unknown. But it may be that Page wanted to reconnect with Samuel F. B. Morse.[4] At the time, Morse, then forty-eight, was developing a working telegraph machine. His goal was to send a signal over a wire from one city to another. (He succeeded a few years later.) Morse was also a gifted painter. Page had been one of his art students.

Page and Mathew Brady arrived in New York late in 1839 or perhaps early in 1840. Shortly before, Morse had returned from Paris. There, he had met with another inventor-artist, Louis Daguerre. Morse was thrilled at Daguerre's latest invention. It was a thin copper plate coated with silver. When exposed to sunlight, the plate recorded an image of whatever rested in front of Daguerre's simple camera.

Called "Boulevard du Temple," the photo that Louis Daguerre took in 1838 or 1839 in Paris was the first photo of a person. At the time, usually anything that moved in a photo would not show up or would be blurry, which is why the carriage traffic on the road cannot be seen. However, the man in the lower left corner was standing still while having his boots polished. So, he became part of history!

Once back in New York, Morse devised his own camera. He then bought a copper plate at a local hardware store. Though these devices were crude, he got impressive results. "I obtained a good [photograph] of the Church of the Messiah, then on Broadway," Morse later wrote.[5]

Soon the inventor teamed up with another early pioneer of photography. Morse's friend, scientist John W. Draper, had also been influenced by Daguerre's work. Draper made improvements on Morse's camera. Late in 1839, Draper created one of the earliest portrait photos. The subject was his sister, Dorothy. She posed outside on a bright sunny day. Yet the equipment was so slow that it took twenty minutes to record her image on the plate. Draper displayed the resulting photo in public a few months later.

The Cutting Edge of a New Art

Later in life, Mathew Brady realized how fortunate he had been as a teenager. Put simply, he had been in the right place at the right time. Only a handful of Americans were then experimenting with cameras and photographic plates. Of these, Morse and Draper were by far the most advanced and successful. And thanks to Page, Mathew Brady met both men. "I was introduced to Morse," Brady recalled. "He had a loft in his brother's storeroom at Nassau and Beekman Streets." Among the fascinating devices in the studio was "an embryo [early] camera."[6]

Through his association with Morse, Mathew Brady got to know Draper. Well before Draper displayed his sister's portrait in public, he showed it to Mathew. The younger man was hugely impressed.

Also during this period, Mathew met a third pioneer of early photography. His name was John Plumbe. A man of exceptional vision, he had a daring passion for large-scale enterprises. For example, he was one of the first people to suggest building a railroad across North America.[7]

John W. Draper took this photo of his sister, Dorothy, in 1839.

The first camera to be sold to the public was designed by Louis Daguerre. It recorded a 6½ x 8½-inch image on a metal plate.

Plumbe also recognized the great financial potential of portrait photography. When the picture of Dorothy Draper went on display in March 1840, he wasted no time. Only a few months later, he opened a photography studio in Washington, D.C. He called it the Plumbe National Daguerrean Gallery. (The term "Daguerrean" referred to Louis Daguerre. In these early years of photography, people routinely called photos on metal plates "daguerreotypes" in his honor. "Gallery," a word borrowed from the art world, was then the common term for a photography studio.) This was only the beginning for Plumbe. He rapidly created the world's first chain of photography studios.

Thus, Mathew Brady came to know several of the trailblazers of photography. The young man likely received lessons in that art at Morse's studio in the early 1840s. Brady also took advice from Draper during these years. And Plumbe's successful galleries almost certainly inspired Brady to open his own when he had the chance.

The Only Place to Live

Morse and the other pioneering photographers were not the only influences on Brady after his move to New York City. The city itself also profoundly influenced him. New York was as unique and colorful then as it is now. And it fascinated the young man. Life there was far faster paced and exciting than what Brady had known growing up in the countryside. One of Brady's modern biographers, James D. Horan, calls New York at that time a "feverish, filthy, mushrooming metropolis."[8]

Brady was captivated and inspired most by the "mushrooming" aspect of New York. At the time, it had a steadily expanding population of about three hundred thousand. The central avenue was Broadway. Stretching for more than three miles, it was lined with thousands of shops and other businesses. Clearly, Brady realized, a person with ambition could make his fortune here. As Horan puts it, "New York was strident, bustling, and alive." For a young man "bursting with dreams and hopes, it was the only place to live."[9]

The Earliest Cameras

An early camera existed long before Brady, Morse, and Daguerre were born. Called a camera obscura, it projected images people could view. But it could not produce permanent images, now called photos.

The camera obscura (meaning "dark chamber") consisted of a darkened room. Light entered from a small hole in one wall. The light cast the image of the scene outside onto the opposite wall. Eventually, people began using a smaller, portable version. It was a wooden box with a hole, or aperture, drilled in one side. Light entered, passed through a lens, and focused an image on a small glass screen. Artists often used the device as an aid in doing sketches.

True photography was not introduced until 1826. A French inventor, Joseph N. Niepce, made the breakthrough. He replaced the glass screen in his camera obscura with a specially-coated metal plate. After at least eight hours, the light entering the camera recorded a permanent image into the plate. It was the world's first photograph.

His First Paying Job

The exact place where Brady lived in his first years in New York is unknown. It may have been located on Chambers Street. That roadway ran (and still runs) from Broadway westward toward the Hudson River. He probably shared a rented room there with his friend William Page.

It was also during this period that Brady landed his first paying job. He worked as a clerk at a well-known department store—A.T. Stewart and Company. It was situated on lower Broadway. Stewart was a smart, enterprising man. He had opened the store in 1823, around the time of Brady's birth. By the time Brady began working there, it was one of the most successful businesses in New York. (Stewart eventually earned $2 million a year, an enormous fortune at the time.)

Brady liked Stewart and enjoyed working for him. (The two remained friends until Stewart's death in 1876.) But the younger man was just as ambitious and hard working as his boss. And Brady soon decided to start his own business. At first, he made and sold small wooden cases for surgical instruments. But soon he began modifying some of them.

From working with Morse and Draper, he saw that cases were needed to hold the finished photographic plates. Reportedly, Brady's photo cases were elegant and attractive. He may have manufactured and sold them in a small shop. A New York business directory printed in 1843 lists a business in his name on Fulton Street, near lower Broadway.[10]

An Industry With Potential

However, Brady viewed making cases strictly as a means to an end. On the one hand, it allowed him to pay his rent and buy food. But more importantly, he was able to save money to finance a different career. He had learned a great deal about photography from Morse and Draper. He felt ready to open his own photo portrait gallery, as John Plumbe had.

Several such galleries had recently opened in New York. All of them were thriving. People were clearly enthralled by the notion of capturing their images on metal plates. Also, at the time, one could have a portrait done for as little as twenty-five to fifty cents, the equivalent of five to fourteen dollars today. The service was quite affordable for all but the very poor.

Thus, Brady saw that he could make a lot of money from photography. He also realized that it could be an excellent outlet for his creative energies. In the fall of 1844, therefore, he decided to open his own gallery. He dreamed of becoming successful, of course. But no one could have predicted how fast this would happen. He was only about twenty-one. Yet within a year he would be one of the most famous people in the country.

Chapter 3

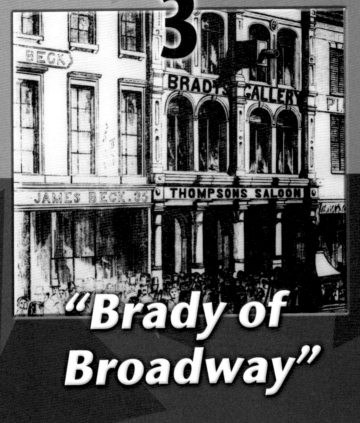

"Brady of Broadway"

Mathew Brady opened his first photo portrait gallery in the fall of 1844. This was a bold move at the time. It was not only because he was so young and had limited business experience. There was also the sheer enormity of his competition. At the time, several new photo galleries opened in New York City each year. (By 1850, only six years later, the documented total was seventy-one galleries. They were staffed by 127 camera operators. By 1858, the number of galleries in the city had risen to two hundred.[1]) Most of these galleries

Historians are not sure when this early daguerreotype of Brady was taken.

were small and produced photos of average to poor quality. But at least half a dozen were large and did high-quality work.

Still, Brady was not deterred. Brimming with confidence and energy, he was determined to make a name for himself. To succeed, he realized, he had to be different from other photographers. Or at least he must *appear* to be different. His strategy was to make his gallery as large and luxurious as possible. That, he hoped, would attract large numbers of customers. Grandness and comfort would also appeal to well-to-do and famous people. And such people could be counted on to pay handsomely for his services.

The fact that Brady's first gallery was so big and plush raises an important question. Where did he get the money to open it? Clearly, some of it came from his savings. But that would have been only a fraction of what was needed. Brady had to have had a backer. He never revealed who this person was. But most historians suspect that his former boss, A. T. Stewart, provided the funds. Stewart was not only rich. He also admired Brady and strongly believed in the young's man's abilities.

A Choice Location

Whoever the backer was, his belief in Brady was not misplaced. When the gallery opened, it delivered on all the promises Brady had made. In fact, it was an instant success. This was partly because of its location. Its young owner wisely chose a spot in the city's choicest business district. The gallery was at the corner of

Brady's gallery was in the heart of New York City.

Broadway and Fulton streets. There were two entrances. The main one—in the front of the three-story red-brick structure—had the address 205 Broadway. A sign, lettered in gold, read: *Brady's Miniature Daguerrean Gallery.* The side entrance was at 162½ Fulton Street. Brady urged celebrities to use it. That way, he said, they could better maintain some measure of privacy.[2]

When an average customer approached the Broadway entrance, he or she saw glass cases on each side. These held recent examples of Brady's photos. After entering the building, the customer took note of a painted sign. It indicated that the gallery was three flights up. At the time, almost all photo galleries, or at least the studios themselves, were located on the top floors of buildings. This allowed the operators the fullest access to sunlight. Electric lights did not yet exist. So photography was completely dependent on sunlight. In fact, on very cloudy days, with minimal sunlight, most early photo galleries closed down.

Upon reaching Brady's gallery on the third story, the customer first entered a reception room. Like the gallery's other rooms, it was richly decorated and elegant. The walls were covered by the owner's own photos, all set in expensive frames. Here, Brady himself often greeted the customer. Fortunately, a description of the young photographer from this period has survived. A reporter for the *New York World*, George A. Townsend, visited the gallery. (It was Townsend who later conducted the 1891 interview with Brady.) He described his host as "a medium-sized, fine-looking young man, about five-feet seven or eight inches tall.

This interior view of Brady's reception gallery shows men and women conversing and looking at his work on the walls of his studio. In the distant background, seen through the entrance to another room, is an operator standing beside a camera. Brady used this woodcut in his ads in Norton's Literary Gazette *in 1854 and in other publications.*

[He had] a sensitive face. [And he had] curly black hair any woman would have envied. A gray, broad-rimmed felt hat gave him the look of a Paris art student."[3]

Lighting, Cameras, and Props

After meeting Brady, the customer entered the "operating room." It was a large chamber equipped with several cameras. Each device was a different size. A large camera made large pictures, while a small camera made small ones. This was because photographers did not yet have equipment that could enlarge or reduce a given photo.

Several skylights were in the operating room's ceiling. Each was about twenty feet long and three feet wide. Movable shades attached to the skylights varied the light levels in the room. Brady had gotten the idea of the skylights and shades from his mentors Morse and Draper. Various mirrors and screens on the floor provided extra brightness control. Like so many others, a New York writer of the day, Charles E. Lester, was impressed. He remarked that Brady had reached an advanced "stage in the art" of photography. "The light shed upon the picture" being taken "seems to be entirely under his control."[4]

Once the light levels were satisfactory, it was time to pose the subject. Brady and the customer discussed which pose would be most appropriate. It had to be one that was easy to maintain for a minute or so. That is how long it took the image to form on the metal plate. Brady told the subject to remain as still as possible during the exposure. Of course, people could not help but blink. But Brady had learned from Morse and Draper that blinking during the process was acceptable. A person's eye was closed for only a tiny fraction of the total exposure time. So the blinking movements were not readily noticeable in the finished picture.

Larger movements were strongly discouraged, however. If the subject moved an arm or leg, for example, it showed up as a blur in the finished photo. So Brady had an array of devices designed to help the person remain still. The subject rested his or her neck against an iron clamp. That kept the head immobile. Meanwhile, a sturdy metal bar kept the subject's back steady. Brady positioned the bar, clamp, and vertical stand that held them behind the subject. Usually the person's body blocked these props from view. However, the stand's metal base was visible in a number of Brady's portrait photos.

The photo's setting often included a decorative carpet, a small table or desk, and a chair. Some subjects stood beside or in front of the furniture. Others posed seated in the chair. Often Brady placed a favorite clock on the table. It was decorated in gold leaf and bore his name on its face.

Brady's Helpers

After Brady had posed the subject, it was time to take the photos. In most cases, however, he himself did not operate the camera. This may have been partly because his eyesight was not very good.[5] He no longer suffered from inflammation of the eyes, as he had in his teens. Still, his eyesight got a little worse each year. And at least by age twenty, he had to wear glasses on a regular basis.

But the main reason Brady did not take many photos was a matter of custom. At the time, owners of the major galleries hired "camera operators." A camera operator prepared the metal plate. Then he inserted it into the camera box. Finally, at Brady's signal, he took the picture.

The camera operator took little or no credit for the finished photo. This was because Brady was the overall boss, both financially and artistically. In some ways, he was similar to a movie producer or director today.

He raised the money to run the gallery. And he both chose its decor and oversaw its daily operation. On the artistic side, he chose which cameras and lenses to use. He also arranged the lighting and posed the subjects. Finally, he kept a close eye on the camera operators to make sure they did things his way.

Nevertheless, Brady's camera operators were skilled technicians. He came to rely on them, and some stayed with him for many years. The first operator he hired may have been James A. Brown.[6] A young, talented artist, Brown definitely was working in the gallery by 1844. Among Brady's other early camera operators were George S. Cook, Austin A. Turner, Thomas Le Mere, Silas Holmes, and Luther Boswell. And almost all of them later went on to become leading photographers.

Tricks of the Trade

One reason Brady's assistants learned so much from him was that he was an innovator. Through trial and error, he invented many tricks of the trade during the 1840s. These became standard techniques as other photographers swiftly adopted them.

For example, he overcame a serious problem caused by white clothing. White shirts, hats, knickers, and so forth reflect light. (In contrast, dark objects absorb light.) So they exposed faster on Brady's plates than dark clothing articles did. Indeed, the white articles quickly became *over*exposed. So they looked much too bright in the finished photos. To counter this problem, Brady covered the white articles with dark cloth during part of the exposure. Partway into the exposure, he ordered the camera operator to cover the lens. Then he swiftly draped the dark cloth in the appropriate places. After stepping aside, he told the operator to continue the exposure. And a few minutes later, he repeated the process, this time removing the dark cloth.

Other tricks Brady introduced made his subjects look better in the finished photos. Sunken cheeks sometimes came out looking like shadows, for instance. So in such cases he inserted wads of cotton in the subject's mouth. If the subject's ears stuck out too much, he used wax to paste them back.

> **Charles Lester wrote that no one devoted "so much time and expense" to the development of photography "as Mr. Brady."**

In addition, Brady made strides in the photography process itself. He was the first to expose images on chemically coated ivory, for example. Afterwards he had artists carefully tint the images by hand. This produced the illusion of a color photograph. (Actual color photography did not yet exist.) Charles Lester wrote that no one devoted "so much time and expense" to the development of photography "as Mr. Brady."[7]

A Reputation for Excellence

Thus, the rapid success of Brady's gallery was due to several factors. He had an excellent location. His studio was elegant, impressive, and comfortable. He hired skilled camera operators. He either invented or mastered the latest picture-taking devices and methods. Finally, he was a talented artist with a keen eye for lighting and proper composition. His photos are usually simple looking, yet forceful, even dramatic.

The combination of these advantages made Brady unique for the time. They brought a special quality to his work. This gave him an edge over his competitors. It also inspired frequent good reviews of his work in newspapers and magazines. Less than two years after opening his doors, he had become known as "Brady of Broadway."

Brady's reputation for excellence attracted the well to do and famous to his gallery. He encouraged them to come and made celebrity portraits a large part of his business. In 1845, he photographed the governor of New York, William Bouck. That same year, the renowned novelist James Fenimore Cooper sat for Brady. So did the noted historian William H. Prescott. In 1846, at age twenty-three, Brady did a portrait of future president Millard Fillmore. Portraits of many other famous subjects were completed in the two years that followed. Among them were the U.S. general Winfield Scott and Mormon leader Brigham Young.

An Artist at Heart

Photos of other famous people came to line the walls of Brady's gallery. Yet the fees he made for taking them accounted for only part of his income. He made a great deal of money selling painted versions of them. The fact

Photographing "Old Hickory"

One of the first important photos Brady took after starting his business was of Andrew Jackson. Nicknamed "Old Hickory," Jackson had served as president from 1829 to 1837. But he had had many exploits battling American Indians and as an army general in the War of 1812 before attaining the presidency.

In 1845, Jackson was seventy-eight and gravely ill. He was confined to his bed at his home, the Hermitage, in Tennessee. Brady heard that President Jackson did not have long to live. So the photographer hastily made the trip to Tennessee. When he arrived at the house on April 15, 1845, Brady found his subject very weak and pale. But Jackson bravely rose to the occasion. According to an eyewitness: "When the moment came that he should sit still, he nerved himself up with the same energy that characterized his whole life. And his eye was stern and fixed and full of fire."[8] Jackson died on June 8, 1845, less than two months after the sitting for Brady.

was that he remained a painter at heart. True, he was proud of his photos. But he always felt that as an art form, photography was secondary to painting. In a later letter to Samuel Morse, he called picture taking "an auxiliary," or added tool, "to the artist."[9] This explains why Brady or his artists applied paint to many of his photos. Some of his assistants, notably James Brown, aided him. In fact, such paintings were for many years the premium product Brady's gallery offered. And they helped make him very well-off.

This relatively sudden financial success allowed Brady to live quite well. Probably shortly after his gallery opened, he moved out of his small rented room. In the five or six years that followed, he mostly took luxury rooms in fine hotels.

Brady's favorite hotel was apparently the Astor House. Built in 1836, it was located on Broadway, not far from his gallery. It featured an elegant white facade with huge Roman-style columns. The owner, Charles A. Stetson, had numerous rich and famous guests. And living in the hotel allowed Brady to meet many of them. Well-known and financially comfortable, he could not imagine his life getting any better. But as he would soon learn, his greatest success and happiness were still to come.

At the Height of Success

In many ways, the decade of 1849 to 1859 marked the high point of Mathew Brady's life. During these years his popularity as a photographer soared. The first major episode was the opening of his first Washington, D.C., gallery late in 1848. The gallery was located near the corner of Pennsylvania Avenue and 4½ Street. At age twenty-five, Brady was already quite famous. So it is not surprising that his services were immediately in demand. Charles Lester remarked: "Brady in Washington was treated with courtesy and attention by the most distinguished men."[1]

In fact, a major reason Brady opened his Washington studio was to gain access to well-known people. He still vigorously pursued his strategy of photographing the rich and famous. This was partly to ensure his own success, of course. But there was also a less commercial aspect to such work. Brady recognized that these photos represented a slice of history for later generations. In his 1891 interview, he recalled: "From the first I regarded myself as under obligation to my country to preserve the faces of its historic men and mothers."[2]

Among these historic persons whose image Brady captured in Washington was President James K. Polk. In January 1849, the photographer formally requested the sitting. He knew that Polk would be leaving office in March. At that time, the newly elected chief executive, Zachary Taylor, would assume power. Brady urgently wanted to photograph Polk while he was still residing at the White House. And he was delighted when Polk agreed to sit for him.

Brady captured this image of President James K. Polk. Polk was president during the Mexican War.

Brady lugged one of his cameras and some plates to the White House on February 14, 1849. He later recorded his first impression of Polk. Adversely affected by the weight of high office, the president looked tired and grim. "His face was lined on both sides of his nose," Brady said. "And his mouth [was] drawn in a tight line."[3] The younger man asked Polk which room had the best natural light. After thinking about it, the president led him to one of the White House dining rooms.[4]

Photographing a Legend

Later that same year, Brady did a portrait of Polk's successor, Zachary Taylor. In fact, all the members of Taylor's cabinet sat for portraits. Some were taken at Brady's Washington gallery. He obtained the others from sittings conducted at the White House. These photos were later combined, by cutting and pasting, into a single group pose. Taylor stood in the middle of the group. This work was truly historic. It was the first time that a U.S. president and his cabinet had been captured by a camera. Brady was proud of this and sent engravings of the photos to Charles G. Bennett, editor of the *New York Herald*. On seeing them, Bennett joked: "Why man, do Washington and his cabinet look like that? Alas, they were dead before my time."[5] (Bennett was humorously comparing Taylor and his cabinet to the first president, George Washington, and his own chief assistants.) Brady delighted in the remark and repeated it frequently in later years.

At top, Brady made this composite using photos of President Zachary Taylor and his Cabinet. From left to right are William Ballard Preston, secretary of the Navy; Thomas Ewing, secretary of the Interior; John Middleton Clayton, secretary of State; Taylor; William Morris Meredith, secretary of the Treasury; George Washington Crawford, secretary of War; Jacob Collamer, postmaster general; and Reverdy Johnson, attorney general. At the bottom is an illustration modeled after the photograph.

As it turned out, Brady was fortunate to capture Taylor's likeness when he did. The president died unexpectedly the following year. Millard Fillmore succeeded him. Brady photographed the new president shortly afterward. It was the second time Fillmore had sat for him.

While in Washington, Brady also had the honor of meeting and photographing a true legend. Dolley Madison, wife of the fourth president, James Madison,

Brady took a photo of President Millard Fillmore. This was the second time the notable American sat for Brady.

had become a heroine during the War of 1812. When the invading British entered the capital, most people fled right away. But she remained in the White House long enough to rescue her husband's papers and a priceless painting of George Washington. Soon after her departure, the British burned the building.

Now eighty, she remained a leading and beloved figure in Washington society. Brady photographed her at her home, not far from the rebuilt White House. Once more, his timing was fortunate. Dolley Madison died a few months later.

Dolley Madison sat for this portrait shortly before she died. She was known in Washington, D.C., for her hospitality during her time as a first lady.

His "Happiest Moment"

Not long after his encounter with the former first lady, Brady met another woman he found extraordinary. Her name was Juliette Elizabeth Handy. Family and friends called her Julia. Her father, Samuel Handy, was a wealthy Maryland lawyer. He had sat for Brady in the Washington gallery. Through him, Brady had met Julia.

Almost nothing specific is known about their courtship. Many decades later, some of Julia's descendents passed on a family tradition about it. They

The Reluctant Poet

Both President Taylor and Dolley Madison died very soon after Brady took their pictures. The same thing happened with the famous poet Edgar Allan Poe. "I had great admiration for Poe," Brady recalled in his 1891 interview.[6]

Another poet, William Ross Wallace, brought Poe to Brady's New York gallery. Brady offered to photograph Poe. But Poe refused. "He thought it was going to cost him something," the photographer later quipped.[7] But when Brady offered to do it for free, Poe gave in. The author of the immortal poem "The Raven" died only a few months later.

told Brady's biographer James Horan that the young couple enjoyed going to parties. The "happiest moment" of Brady's life, Horan writes, "was on the evening when he took Julia into his arms." They "glided across the [dance] floor to the strains of a beautiful waltz."[8]

The exact date of the couple's wedding is also unknown. A few surviving newspaper clippings suggest that it was late in 1849 or early in 1850. According to the National Portrait Gallery, it took place in 1851. More certain than the year is that the marriage took place at the East Street Baptist Church in Washington.

Brady made sure to take a picture of the minister, George W. Samson.

After their marriage, Mathew and Julia Brady moved into Washington's fashionable National Hotel. They appear to have led a quiet, happy life. They had no children. But both came to love and spend time with her brother's son, Levin Handy. Julia was genuinely interested in her husband's work. She visited him at his galleries on a regular basis. In one such visit, Brady took a family portrait. He stood, while Julia and her sister (whose name is known only as Mrs. Haggerty) sat in front of him.

A Volume of Noted Americans

As it turned out, Brady and his new bride did not stay long in the nation's capital. At some point in 1850, he got into a dispute about money with the landlord of his Washington gallery. They could not reach an agreement, so Brady closed the gallery. He and his wife returned to New York and moved into the Astor House.

That same year, Brady published a book. For years he had been compiling photos of famous people. He had long considered converting some to engravings and using them in a book. An engraving was made by etching, or cutting, a picture or design into a wooden or metal surface. Sometimes people engraved images onto a sheet of copper. They then coated the copper with ink and pressed a piece of paper to it. The image created this way was also called an engraving. Brady felt that using engravings in the book would give it a classy look.

Brady poses with his wife, Julia Brady, left, and her sister, Mrs. Haggerty.

This is because engraving had long been seen as a stylish, elegant art form.

Brady titled the volume *The Gallery of Illustrious Americans*. It contained the likenesses of twelve people. Among them were five noted politicians, Henry Clay, John C. Calhoun, Lewis Cass, Daniel Webster, and Silas Wright. There were also renderings of presidents Taylor and Fillmore. A famous author, William E. Channing, was included. And the book showed two renowned military generals, John C. Fremont and Winfield Scott. The historian William H. Prescott and artist and naturalist John J. Audubon rounded out the volume.

The portraits in the book were engravings based on Brady's original photos of the twelve men. His publisher, Francis D'Avignon, personally did the engravings. Charles Lester, by now one of Brady's closest friends, wrote a short text describing the book's subjects. In the foreword, he wrote: "In preparation for this book, no department has been neglected. Mr. Brady has been [for] many years collecting portraits. . . . His reputation in his art has been too long established to need commendation [praise]."[9]

The finished volume today would be categorized as a coffee-table book. It weighed five pounds and sold for thirty dollars. That was a great deal of money for any book at the time. *The Gallery of Illustrious Americans* received excellent reviews. However, it was not the big financial success its author had hoped for. Still, Brady profited handsomely from it in other ways. It made him even more famous than he had already been. It also increased the volume of his business. Thousands of people made appointments at his gallery. They hoped to have their portraits done by the country's leading photographer.

Success in Europe

Brady enjoyed still more success the following year. In 1851, Queen Victoria and the British government sponsored the first World's Fair. It was called The Great Exhibition of the Works of Industry of All Nations. Its purpose was to celebrate and promote industrial progress. Most of the exhibits were housed in an enormous structure made of glass panels. It was appropriately named the Crystal Palace. Prizes were given for the most impressive exhibits in each category.

One category recognized the new industry and art of photography. Photographers from six countries— England, France, Austria, Germany, Italy, and the United States—entered their works. Most were still using standard daguerreotypes, as Brady was. But some were clearly more skilled and imaginative than others. Confident in his own skills, Brady chose forty-eight of what he considered his best photos. He mailed them to the Great Exhibition's officials in London.

Soon afterward, on July 12, 1851, Mathew and Julia Brady boarded a ship bound for England. During the voyage, he looked forward to seeing Europe for the first time. Brady was particularly eager to meet one of his personal heroes—Louis Daguerre. It was not until the couple arrived in London that they learned that

Daguerre had died on the very day they left from New York.

Though saddened by the news, Brady's mood soon brightened. He and his photos became a huge hit at the Great Exhibition. American photographers won all the prizes in their category. M. M. Lawrence got a prize for creating a large (10.5 X 12.5 inches) daguerreotype portrait. Another award went to John A. Whipple for taking photos of the moon. But Brady received the biggest prize of all, for "overall mastery of the medium of photography."[10] It therefore honored the excellence of his larger body of work.

Following the exhibition, Brady and his wife toured France and Italy. He was delighted to discover that he was well known in artistic circles throughout Europe. In his 1891 interview, he stated: "That year I went through the galleries of Europe and found my pictures everywhere as far as Rome and Naples." Moreover, years later a number of prominent Europeans remembered his work and sought out his services. "When in 1860 [some British nobles] came to America," Brady recalled:

> **"I went through the galleries of Europe and found my pictures everywhere as far as Rome and Naples."**

I was surprised, amidst much competition [among photo galleries], that they came to my gallery and repeatedly sat. So I said to the Duke of Newcastle: "Your Grace, might I ask to what I owe your favor to my studio? I am at a loss to understand your kindness." "Are you not the Mr. Brady," he said, "who earned the prize nine years ago in London?"[11]

Four New Galleries

The fame gained by his book and the prize he received in London made Brady more successful than ever. But with fame and success came increasing demand for his services. And he found that his New York gallery was unable to keep up with that demand.

So he decided to open a second gallery in that city. It opened in March 1853. Located at 359 Broadway, it was beautifully decorated. The photography magazine *Humphrey's Journal* printed a description of the lavish reception room:

> *This room is about twenty-six by forty feet and is the largest reception room in this city. The floors are carpeted with superior velvet tapestry. . . . The walls are covered with satin and gold paper. . . . Suspended on the walls, we find [photos] of presidents, generals, kings, queens, [and] noblemen.*[12]

At first, Brady tried to manage both galleries himself by spending part of each day in each. But as time went on, it became clear that this was both exhausting and inefficient. So in 1856 he hired a talented Scottish photographer named Alexander Gardner. Gardner oversaw the photographic sessions that Brady was too busy to attend. Gardner was also a skilled businessman. Thereafter he largely managed the business, which allowed Brady to spend more time promoting the galleries.

An added bonus was that Gardner had recently mastered a new photography process. Invented by an Englishman, Frederick S. Archer, it used glass rather than metal plates. The result was a negative image that could be used to make copies. This so-called "wet-plate" process rapidly replaced the older method.

Brady took full advantage of the new photography process. The ability to use glass plates led him and Gardner to produce larger than normal-sized photos. (Before the advent of this process, normal-sized daguerreotypes most often came in three sizes— 6.5 x 8.5 inches, 4.5 x 5.5 inches, and 2 x 2.5 inches.) They called the larger photos "Imperials." These measured 17 by 21 inches at first and became even larger later.

Most often, Brady and his hired artists retouched the Imperials with paint. This allowed him to fetch prices ranging from $50 to $750 each for them. Gardner also urged Brady to take advantage of their new ability to make plentiful copies of their pictures. They began turning out "card photos" of famous people. These were about the size of today's baseball trading cards. And in fact, people traded Brady's cards just as people trade baseball cards today. Brady sold tens of thousands of these cards in the years that followed.

Brady used the wet-plate process at both of his New York galleries. He also employed it at three more

Alexander Gardner was not only a photographer for Brady, but also supervised other photographers. Taken in 1860, this is the earliest known photograph of Gardner.

The Wet-Plate Process

The wet-plate photographic process was introduced in the early 1850s. Its inventor was English sculptor and photographer Frederick S. Archer. He began with a rectangular glass plate. Onto the plate he painted a sticky liquid called collodion. It was a mixture of alcohol, ether, cotton, and sulfuric acid. He then placed the plate in a bath of silver nitrate and put it in his camera and exposed it to light before the collodion dried. (This was the source of the term *wet plate*.) The light interacted with the chemicals, burning an image onto the plate. Because the plate was partly transparent, it could later be used as a negative. Shining light through it onto a specially treated sheet of paper produced a positive print. This initiated the age of photo printing.

Brady owned this wet-plate camera.

galleries he opened in his most successful decade. In January 1858, he inaugurated a new Washington, D.C., gallery. He called it the National Photographic Art Gallery. He put Alexander Gardner in charge of it. About a year later, in 1859, Brady opened a third gallery in New York. And in 1860, he opened a fourth.

One of the first customers at the newest New York gallery was a tall, imposing-looking man from Illinois. Brady was about to take one of his most famous photos. The tall man was none other than Abraham Lincoln.

5

Photographing
Lincoln

Every few years, the leading American historians meet and vote on who they see as the greatest (and worst) U.S. presidents. The sixteenth president—Abraham Lincoln (1809–1865)—always ranks in the top three. They attribute to him two monumental achievements. First, Lincoln managed to keep the country from splitting apart permanently. He was elected president only a few months before the outbreak of the Civil War. And he guided the Union to its ultimate victory in that conflict.

Lincoln's second great achievement was ending slavery. On September 22, 1862, he introduced the Emancipation Proclamation. When it took effect on January 1, 1863, that document began the process of freeing millions of African Americans from slavery.

As Lincoln made history, Mathew Brady occasionally found himself at the great man's side. In fact, in a sense Brady had an indirect role in that history-making. Lincoln himself pointed out Brady's pivotal contribution. The president remarked that a photo Brady had taken of him had helped make his 1860 election victory possible. This, Lincoln said, was because the picture had been so widely reproduced.

Moreover, Brady's many pictures of Lincoln became, collectively, a priceless historical record. Historians estimate that Lincoln sat for thirty-three different photographers. These sessions produced about 126 photos of him. Of these, about 35 were taken by Brady or his employees.

Per custom, in most cases Brady did not take the pictures himself. Rather, he supervised while his camera operators took the photos. For instance, Alexander Gardner took 30 of the 126 photos of Lincoln. Some of these Gardner took while working for Brady. Others were taken later, after Gardner had struck out on his own. (Gardner holds the record. He photographed Lincoln more than any other person.) Some of Brady's photos of Lincoln were taken at Brady's Washington gallery. Another of Brady's assistants, Anthony Berger, photographed Lincoln 13 times. Whichever of his associates was involved, Brady supplied the studio and supervised. So he often received most or all of the credit.

The Cooper Union Photos

The first time Brady met and photographed Lincoln was in February 1860. Brady had recently opened his fourth New York gallery. It was located at the corner of Broadway and Tenth Street. But at the time it was closed for renovations. So the photo session happened at the Brady studio located at the corner of Broadway and Bleecker Street.

Lincoln was then campaigning for the Republican nomination for the presidency. He had originally been scheduled to speak in Brooklyn, several miles from Manhattan. However, he delayed his trip for too long. And his speaking venue was no longer available. So he had to find a new place in the area to speak. Lincoln agreed to speak at the Cooper Union (newspapers and people at the time often incorrectly called it the Cooper Institute) on February 27. It was located on Seventh Street, not far from Brady's Bleecker Street gallery.

Lincoln arrived at the gallery in the morning of February 27. After meeting him, Brady realized that Lincoln would not be easy to photograph. First, he was six foot four in bare feet and stood an inch or two taller wearing shoes. This made it very difficult to take standing photos. To make sure Lincoln's entire body was visible, Brady would have to move the camera backward. As a result, Lincoln's face would be farther away. And less facial detail would be visible. Nevertheless, one of the three pictures Brady took that day was a full-body pose. Some historians think he made this photo for noted sculptor Henry Kirke Brown. Brown later referred to this likeness while fashioning a famous statue of Lincoln.

Brady also noticed that Lincoln's collar and necktie were loose. It not only looked untidy, but made his long neck stand out. Brady later recalled, "When I got him before the camera I asked him if I might not arrange his collar, and with that he began to pull it up." In a friendly tone, Lincoln said, "I see you want to shorten my neck."[1] Grinning, Brady told the other man that this was exactly what he wanted. And they both laughed.

That night, Lincoln gave his speech at the Cooper Union. He spoke out against slavery. Anyone who loved God, he said, must despise that wretched institution.

The next day the speech appeared in newspapers across the country. It aroused a great deal of attention and controversy. Pictures of Lincoln were suddenly in great demand. Brady rose to this challenge. His studios turned out thousands of copies of what became known as the Cooper Union photo. And Lincoln's aides used it often in his campaign. In historian Harold Holzer's words, the Cooper Union photo of Lincoln was:

> . . . the most important single visual record of Lincoln's, or perhaps any American presidential campaign. . . . Its later [wide distribution] and reproduction in prints, medallions, [posters], and banners perhaps did as much to create a "new" Abraham Lincoln as did the Cooper Union speech itself.[2]

This photo of Abraham Lincoln taken before he delivered his Cooper Union address made the presidential hopeful even more famous around the country.

First Official Presidential Photos

The next time that Brady and Lincoln met was on February 24, 1861. Lincoln had been elected president and was preparing for his inauguration. He and his aides decided that Brady should take the new chief executive's first official photos. Accompanied by his security guards, Lincoln went to Brady's Washington gallery. A newspaper reporter witnessed the event. He later wrote that the president-elect "was dressed in plain black clothes." He also sported "black whiskers—and how well trimmed." This was in marked contrast to the unkempt image he had so often displayed in prior months. "Some of the ladies say he is almost good-looking," the reporter joked.[3]

This time Brady was better prepared for his famous client. The photographer realized that he was about to take a truly historic picture. And he naturally wanted everything to be just right. He chose his most trusted associate, Alexander Gardner, to operate the camera. Also, these men wanted to make sure that Lincoln's poses would be as attractive as possible. To that end, Brady called on a friend, George H. Story. He was a respected painter who had a studio on the floor above Brady's gallery.

While Brady and Gardner scurried about, making last-minute lighting adjustments, Story approached Lincoln. The painter was immediately struck by the president-elect's sad expression as he sat in a chair. Lincoln seemed deeply troubled. Surely his taking office as a possible civil war was brewing was weighing on him heavily. "He did not utter a word," Story later commented. "He seemed absolutely indifferent to all that was going on about him. And he gave the impression that he was a man overwhelmed with anxiety and fatigue and care."[4]

Suddenly, as Story watched, Lincoln raised his left hand and stared intently at the floor. The image, while very informal, was nothing less than striking. At that same moment, Brady, now ready to begin, asked Story to pose the subject. "Pose him?" Story blurted out. "Never. Bring the camera and take him as he is!"[5] Brady and Gardner agreed and seized the moment. The photo they snapped is one of the finest ever taken of Lincoln. It beautifully captures certain aspects of his character that have become legendary. As Story himself later put it: "There was a solemnity [calmness] and dignity about him. And [he had] a general air that bespoke weight of character." In addition, Story said, "honesty was written in every line of his face."[6]

As the sitting ended, Brady felt completely satisfied with the results. He may have felt that the historic session could not have gone better for him. If so, he was wrong. At the last moment one of the security guards spoke up. He realized that Brady and Lincoln had not spoken the whole time. The guard assumed the two men had never met. And he tried to introduce Brady to Lincoln. But the president-elect made it clear that he remembered Brady fondly. "[Mr.] Brady and the Cooper Institute made me president," Lincoln said with a smile.[7]

This picture posed by George H. Story, curator-emeritus of the Metropolitan Museum of Art in New York on February 23, 1861, was taken by Brady in the Washington Gallery. It shows Lincoln's sad mood on that day.

Inauguration Day

Following the February encounter with Lincoln, Brady eagerly began preparing for the coming inauguration. It was scheduled for March 4, less than two weeks away. So Brady applied for a special government pass. He asked for clearance to place his cameras very close to the speakers' platform.

Brady was unable to get the pass, however. The chief of presidential security, Allan Pinkerton, was too worried about Lincoln's safety. The ongoing tensions between the North and the South increased the danger of an assassination attempt. So Pinkerton placed sharp-shooters all around the platform. If anyone made a suspicious move toward Lincoln, these men would immediately open fire. In addition, shortly before the ceremonies a rumor claimed someone might plant explosives under the platform.

Therefore, Brady and his assistants could not get near the platform. So the surviving photos taken of the inauguration, showing a gathered crowd listening to Lincoln's speech, are not his. They were taken by Benjamin B. French and Montgomery Meigs.

Later Photos of Lincoln

Brady had more luck photographing the new president in the months and years that followed. Sometime later in 1861 Lincoln returned to Brady's Washington gallery. This time he brought a chair with him. He explained to Brady that this was the chair he had used

Capturing Lincoln's Family

Mathew Brady photographed Abraham Lincoln during the preparations for the 1861 presidential inauguration. During this same period the president-elect's wife, Mary Todd Lincoln, also sat for Brady.

The session with Mrs. Lincoln produced two photos. She did not like the way she appeared in the pictures. And she later asked that the negatives be destroyed. This did not happen, however. Prints continued to sell for years to come.

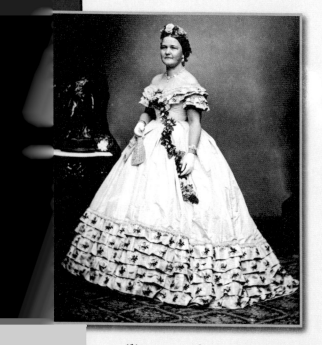

Brady also photographed Lincoln's three living sons, Robert, William, and Tad. (The Lincolns' fourth son, Edward, had died in 1850.) Robert and William posed for Brady in stylish suits. In contrast, Tad wore a military uniform. (William died not long after the photos were taken. Tad died a few years later, at age eighteen.)

in the House of Representatives. (Lincoln had earlier served as a congressman.) Brady's chairs were too small for him, Lincoln said. They were not to his liking and would make posing an uncomfortable experience. So he had brought his own chair. However, the president added, it was now Brady's to keep.

Brady took six photos of Lincoln that day. Again, the president became solemn and moody. It seemed to Brady that this happened every time Lincoln sat for him. And in fact, the president's eldest son, Robert, confirmed it. "When any attempt was made to photograph my father," he later remarked, "he relapsed into his melancholy [sad] mood."[8] In truth, Lincoln had good reason for being sad that day. Some of the southern states had recently seceded from the Union. There was so much turmoil in the capital he had to impose a curfew and other strict rules to help restore order.

Brady and his assistants photographed Lincoln several more times during the ensuing Civil War. One of these sittings took place in the Washington gallery in 1862. Lincoln posed for one of Brady's and Gardner's large Imperials, as well as for other photos. Another session occurred the following year, on April 17, 1863. This was only a few months after Lincoln had issued the Emancipation Proclamation. This time another of Brady's operators, Thomas Le Mere, took the pictures.

Lincoln sat at the Washington gallery still again on February 9, 1864. This session produced some of the most famous photos ever taken of the sixteenth president. Anthony Berger operated the camera on this occasion. Brady supervised, arranged the lighting, and

This image taken of Lincoln by Brady was used later as the basis for the Lincoln penny.

posed the subject. The fruitful session produced eight pictures. One was later used as a model for Lincoln's image on the five-dollar bill. A second was used similarly for his image on the penny.

A third picture taken that day showed the president with his fourth son, Tad. Brady posed the boy, then eleven, with his father. He had both subjects look intently at a large book (a photo album). This picture became widely famous and in demand. Tens of thousands of card photos of it were distributed far and wide. (According to historian Bob Zeller, "Brady generally sold negatives to the E. & H. T. Anthony & Company, which was the firm that duplicated them by the thousands."[9])

Capturing a Crucial Transition

It is somewhat unclear who took the last photos of Lincoln and when. It was long thought that Alexander Gardner did, well after he had parted ways with Brady. A number of scholars think the historic sitting took place on April 10, 1865. This was one day after Confederate general Robert E. Lee surrendered his army. It was also four days before Lincoln was shot.

However, other scholars suggest that Lincoln sat for Gardner on February 5, 1865. They say that the last photos of Lincoln were more likely taken on March 6. If so, the photographer was Henry F. Warren, of Massachusetts.

Either way, Gardner's last photos of Lincoln were historic. One in particular, a close-up, stunningly captured the president's careworn expression. While Gardner was processing the glass plate, it cracked. He managed to make one photo. Then he discarded the plate. Fortunately, the picture survived and was later photocopied.

Neither Gardner, nor Brady, nor Warren, nor anyone else was able to photograph the living Lincoln

President Lincoln and his son, Tad, look at a book in this photo by Brady.

Tad Lincoln's Outburst

Not long after Lincoln sat for Brady on February 9, 1864, an unfortunate event occurred at the White House. At the time, a well-known painter named Francis Carpenter was staying there. He had been asked to do a painting of the president.

To aid in his work, Carpenter requested that Brady take some new photos. So Brady sent two of his assistants to the White House. Carpenter made the mistake of storing some of the men's equipment in Tad Lincoln's bedroom. The boy, who had a bad temper, took offense. He locked Brady's helpers out and refused to open the door.

Upset, Carpenter ran into Lincoln's office to report the mishap. The president went and got the key from his son and unlocked the room, giving Carpenter an apology. "Tad is a peculiar child," Lincoln said with regret.[10]

after April 14, 1865. On that day an assassin, John Wilkes Booth, shot the president at Ford's Theatre, in the capital. Lincoln died the next morning.

Brady was greatly saddened by Lincoln's untimely death. He felt he had gotten to know the president over the years. He also recognized Lincoln's greatness as a leader.

This is the last photo taken of Lincoln by Alexander Gardner. Some historians think it was taken on April 10, 1865, four days before Lincoln was assassinated. However, many now believe it was taken on February 5, 1865.

At the time, there was no way to know if the new president, Andrew Johnson, could fill the old one's shoes. But shortly after Johnson recited the oath of office, Brady took a standing photo of him. In this way, the new art of photography captured a crucial transition in American history.

Chapter

6

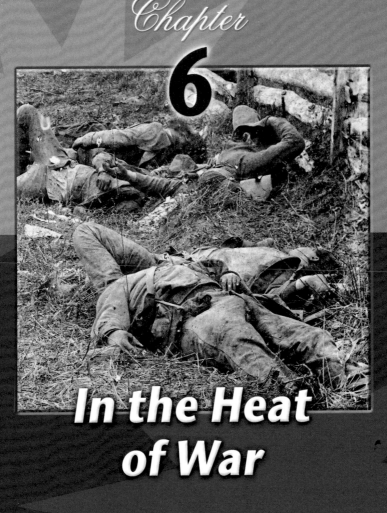

In the Heat
of War

Not long after Mathew Brady first photographed Abraham Lincoln, the American Civil War began. The onset of the conflict affected Brady in two immediate ways. First, early in 1861 his galleries were suddenly busier than ever. In particular, his Washington gallery was swamped with customers. Most were Union soldiers. Tens of thousands of young men from northern states streamed into the nation's capital. Many were eager to have their pictures taken. Souvenir photos of soldiers posing in their uniforms were so popular that photographers could not keep up with the demand.

The second major effect the war had on Brady was to inspire him with the greatest single goal of his career. He saw that photography could do much more than turn out posed portraits. It could also capture the events of a war with stunning realism. On the one hand, he reasoned, the public would clamor to see and buy such photos. On the other, these pictures would form a permanent historical record.

Not all of those close to Brady agreed with this challenging plan. In fact, he later admitted that his wife and closest friends were not very happy about it. Not surprisingly, Julia worried about what might happen to her husband in the heat of battle. She could not bear the thought of his being killed or wounded. But she soon saw that his mind was made up.

Many Union soldiers and officers came to Brady's Washington, D.C., studio to have their pictures taken before they went off to war. This unidentified person was a Union officer.

Preparing for Battle

Brady knew that civilians were not normally allowed in battle zones. So he would need to get a special military pass to accompany the soldiers to Bull Run. To this end, he went to see Winfield Scott, then chief of the Army. The two were acquainted, since Brady had photographed the aging general years before. In confidence, Scott told his visitor that he would no longer be leading the troops toward Bull Run. Brigadier General Irvin McDowell now had that duty. So Brady hurried to see McDowell, who issued him the important pass.

Brady realized from the start that he could not tackle such an immense project by himself. He managed to assemble an impressive team of photographers. Among its members were Alexander Gardner and Timothy O'Sullivan, both from his Washington gallery. Gardner's talented brother James also joined the team. So did David Knox, James Gibson, George Barnard, William Pywell, David Woodbury, Guy Fowx, and John Wood. Brady hired other camera operators as well. In the nineteenth-century book *The Camera and Pencil*, Marcus A. Root wrote: "Brady photographed [the war] having eighteen or twenty assistants employed on the work for months."[1]

All of these men required cameras and tripods, of course. Moreover, each field photographer needed a wagon containing a mobile darkroom. (Darkrooms were needed because natural light ruins developing photos.) It had to be light-tight while the collodion on the glass plates was still wet. So Brady and his assistants carefully

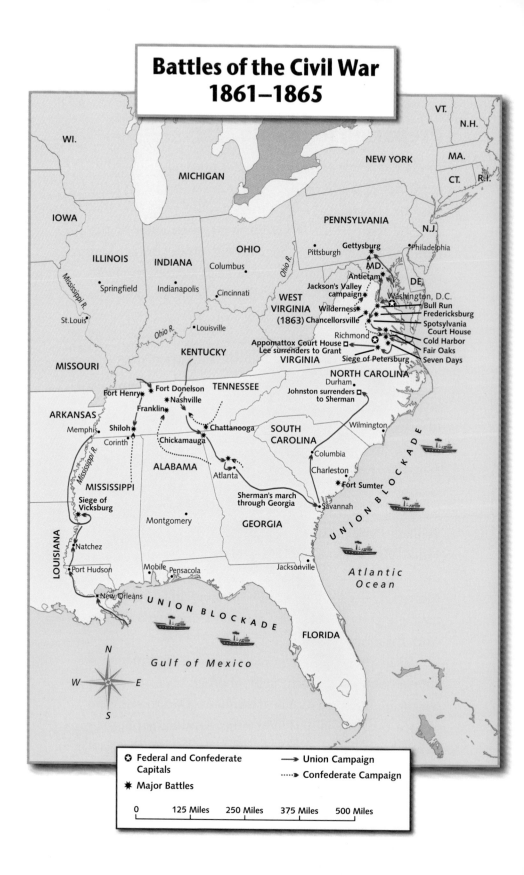

Battles of the Civil War 1861–1865

VT.
N.H.
MA.
CT. R.I.

NEW YORK

WI.

MICHIGAN

IOWA

PENNSYLVANIA

N.J.

ILLINOIS

INDIANA

OHIO

Pittsburgh   Gettysburg   • Philadelphia

Columbus •

Springfield   • Indianapolis   • Cincinnati

Ohio R.

MD.
Antietam
Jackson's Valley
campaign
Washington, D.C.   Bull Run
WEST   Fredericksburg
VIRGINIA   Wilderness   Spotsylvania
(1863)   Chancellorsville   Court House
Cold Harbor
Richmond   Fair Oaks
Appomattox Court House ☐   Seven Days
Lee surrenders to Grant   Siege of Petersburg
VIRGINIA

DE.

St.Louis •

Mississippi R.

Ohio R.   • Louisville

MISSOURI

KENTUCKY

TENNESSEE

NORTH CAROLINA

Fort Henry ✱   ✱ Fort Donelson
✱ Nashville
Franklin ✱

Durham •
Johnston surrenders ☐
to Sherman

ARKANSAS

Memphis •   Shiloh ✱
Corinth •

✱ Chattanooga
Chickamauga

SOUTH
CAROLINA

Wilmington •

Mississippi R.

ALABAMA

Atlanta

Columbia •
Charleston •

U N I O N   B L O C K A D E

MISSISSIPPI
Siege of
Vicksburg

Montgomery •

Sherman's march
through Georgia

✱ Fort Sumter

• Savannah

GEORGIA

LOUISIANA   • Natchez

• Port Hudson   Mobile • Pensacola •

• Jacksonville

Atlantic
Ocean

• New Orleans   U N I O N   B L O C K A D E

FLORIDA

N
W   E
S

Gulf of Mexico

✪ Federal and Confederate
Capitals

✱ Major Battles

→ Union Campaign

····▶ Confederate Campaign

0   125 Miles   250 Miles   375 Miles   500 Miles

wrapped thick sheets of canvas around the work space. That kept light from entering. Brady also made sure that each mobile darkroom was equipped with the required chemicals and workbenches. (The equipment and supplies Brady bought were expensive. This was not the last time he would spend huge amounts of money in hopes of achieving success.)

At first, the field darkrooms used by Brady and other war photographers had no special name. But as time went on, curious soldiers repeatedly asked, "What is it?" when they saw one. So they came to be called "what's-it wagons."[2]

Living With Limitations

In some ways, therefore, Brady and his assistants were well prepared. However, they still had to live with some severe limitations and problems. First, their sealed what's-it wagons became very hot inside during the summer months. Also, the stench of collodion and other chemicals inside was thick. So the workers sometimes became light-headed or ill during the development process.

In addition, the wagons were heavy and slow. So it took a long time to reach the sites of key battles. When possible, the photographers overcame this obstacle by taking advantage of local rivers. They loaded the wagons onto rafts and floated them downstream. The slowness of the wagons also kept them from swiftly fleeing dangerous situations. This is why one of Brady's wagons overturned at the first battle of Bull Run in July 1861.

A more fundamental and serious limitation existed in the photography process itself. The wet-plate method worked much faster than the old metal-plate method. But exposures of two to ten seconds were still necessary to achieve a sharp, clear picture. That meant that capturing moving people or objects was difficult or impossible. Any sudden movement showed up as a ghost-like blur on the final photo.

Thus, for the most part during the war, Brady and his helpers concentrated on stationary subjects. They produced numerous shots of buildings and city streets, for example. One of the most striking is a wide view of the ruins of the Confederate capital, Richmond. (Most of the city burned in 1865.) Brady's assistants also took numerous photos of people. Some were soldiers in Union camps, on the roads, or in towns. Others were civilians in various situations. Most of these pictures were posed. At the photographer's request, the subject or subjects stood as still as possible for several seconds. Brady and his assistants also took dozens of photos of dead bodies during the conflict.

The Antietam Photos

In fact, Brady was long credited, incorrectly, with personally producing some of the most graphic and moving photos of Civil War dead. These were the soldiers killed on what came to be known as America's bloodiest day. The battle of Antietam was fought in

A man stands on a shoreline overlooking the ruins of Richmond in this Brady photo.

mid-September 1862. It is also called the battle of Sharpsburg because it took place near Sharpsburg, Maryland. On one side were about 87,000 Union troops led by General George B. McClellan. On the other were some 45,000 Confederate soldiers under General Robert E. Lee. Of these forces, more than 2,100 Union troops died in the battle. And Lee lost more than 1,540 men.[3]

A series of photos of these dead soldiers did in fact go on display in one of Brady's New York galleries three weeks later. He called the collection "The Dead of Antietam." The gruesome photos boldly confronted the public with the horrors of the war. *The New York Times* summed up the collection's impact this way:

> *Mr. Brady has done something to bring home to us the terrible reality and earnestness of war. If he has not brought bodies and laid them on our dooryard and along the streets, he has done something very like it. . . . These pictures have a terrible distinctness. . . . We would scarce choose to be in the gallery when one of the women bending over them should recognize a husband, a son, or a brother in the still, lifeless lines of bodies.*[4]

This and other similar public commentary was misleading, however. Brady's presentation of the photos made it look as if he had gone to the Antietam battlefield himself and overseen the photography. In reality, he had not. Brady remained in New York and sent Alexander Gardner and James Gibson to Antietam.

There, Gardner and Gibson took one hundred photos, mostly on September 19 and 20.[5]

These two men made sure to copyright the pictures they had taken at Antietam. Their names appeared in very tiny print along the lower front edge of the photos that were released to the public. But as William Frassanito points out, "few people took the trouble of reading the fine print. And all the attention instead was drawn to the words, 'Brady's Album Gallery,' prominently displayed on each identifying label."

That Brady took most of the credit for the photos was neither surprising nor unusual. This was "not an uncommon practice at the time," Frassanito says. "Most large firms then in the business of photographing

Bodies lie near a fence at the Antietam battlefield in September 1862. The camera operator for this Brady photo was Alexander Gardner.

scenes for the mass market rarely mentioned the names of individual cameramen."[6]

Mounting Financial Troubles

Though this practice was common, it sometimes caused bad feelings between Brady and his assistants. Gardner, for instance, appears to have resented it. "It must have irritated Gardner," Frassanito writes. The Scottish photographer did not like "to see Brady receive credit for the most sensational series of war photographs yet presented to the American public."[7]

Eventually, Gardner decided he would be better off running his own photography studio. Sometime between November 1862 and May 1863, he left Brady.[8] The exact date the two men parted company is unknown. What is certain is that Gardner opened his own photographic gallery in Washington, D.C., in May 1863. His brother James came to work for him. So did Timothy O'Sullivan and some other key Brady employees. Brady replaced Gardner with James Gibson, who became manager of Brady's gallery in the capital.

These events took a financial toll on Brady. First, in addition to personnel, Gardner took business away from him. Also, Gibson lacked Gardner's administrative skills. So it was not long before Brady's gallery began losing money. This setback, coupled with what he was spending to photograph the war, caused his debts to mount rapidly. Shortly after Gardner left, Gibson left Brady as well and went to work for Gardner.

Tom Thumb's Wedding

Photographing troops and battles did not occupy all of Mathew Brady's time during the Civil War. In fact, overall he spent more time in Washington and New York than he did in the field. And he continued to photograph people and events unrelated to the war.

Perhaps the most famous of these events was the wedding of Charles Sherwood Stratton—better known by his stage name, Tom Thumb. He stood just two feet nine inches tall. Stratton was a major attraction in the circus run by the leading showman of the time, P. T. Barnum. Always looking for publicity, P. T. Barnum advertised Stratton's marriage to another little person, Lavinia Warren.

The ceremony, which took place early in 1863, drew huge crowds in New York City. Brady was the official wedding photographer. The card photos he made of the couple sold by the tens of thousands.

Brady at Gettysburg

Brady remained hopeful that his financial situation would improve. So he continued to photograph the war. One of his most memorable accomplishments was photographing the site of the conflict's most famous battle. The battle took place on July 1, 2, and 3, 1863, at Gettysburg, in eastern Pennsylvania. In this Union victory, a total of 5,662 Union and Confederate soldiers were killed and 27,703 were wounded.[9]

Both Brady and Gardner hastened to photograph the Gettysburg battlefield. Gardner, accompanied by

Mathew Brady posed for his portrait along a fence, staring out at McPherson's Woods, where General John F. Reynolds had fallen to a Confederate sniper's bullet. Brady instructed the camera operator to expose a series of negatives to create this wide shot, called a panorama.

James Gibson and Timothy O'Sullivan, arrived first, probably late on July 5.[10] These men were in time to take pictures of the dead before they were buried.

Brady and his assistants, David B. Woodbury and Anthony Burger, did not make it to Gettysburg until July 15.[11] They were too late to photograph any dead bodies. So they concentrated on recording various landmarks in the area. These included Lee's headquarters during the battle; Culp's Hill, a key Union defensive position; Little Round Top, site of an unsuccessful Confederate charge; and the town of Gettysburg itself. They also took a picture of Confederate prisoners that is praised by historians today. In all, the team compiled about thirty pictures over the course of two or three days.

Brady took this famous photo of Confederate prisoners after the Battle of Gettysburg.

These photos were among the finest and most important taken during the entire Civil War. "Though lacking in the dramatic impact of Gardner's," Frassanito remarks, they "nevertheless serve as an invaluable and unique guide to the field's appearance during the month of the battle."[12] Indeed, says historian Bob Zeller, Brady and Gardner "complemented one another's work" at Gettysburg. "Brady's wide-screen vision was one perspective; Gardner's hard-news [approach] was quite another. For history's sake, the breakup [between the two men] was all for the best."[13]

Photographing Grant

In the months after he returned from Gettysburg, Brady spent a great deal of time at his galleries. To maintain his reputation, he still catered to famous people whenever possible. Among the more renowned individuals who sat for Brady in the last year of the war was Ulysses S. Grant. (President Lincoln gave Grant control of the federal military in March 1864.)

Grant showed up at Brady's Washington gallery on March 9, 1864. "I had the studio in readiness early," Brady later recalled. "We waited long after one o'clock, and had almost given him up." But then "a carriage drove up and Secretary of War [Edwin] Stanton jumped out, followed hurriedly by Grant."[14]

Stanton and Grant explained that they could not stay long. They urgently had to catch a train in a little over an hour. So Brady dutifully did his job as quickly as he could. He managed to get four excellent photos of

General Grant posed for four portraits in Brady's Washington Gallery.

On the Brink of Changing History

Brady experienced some hair-raising incidents during the Civil War. One of the most memorable took place not on a battlefield, but in his own studio. It happened on March 9, 1864.

Ulysses S. Grant had just arrived at Brady's Washington gallery. Grant sat down, preparing to be photographed. Brady had earlier asked one of his assistants to adjust the shade on the glass skylight above. Suddenly, the man slipped, fell, and crashed through the glass. Large glass shards rained down around the general.

Fortunately, Grant was not injured. "It was a miracle that some of the pieces didn't strike him," Brady later remarked. "And if one did, it would have been the end of Grant, for that glass was two inches thick!"[15] Surely, if Grant had died that day, history would have been very different.

his subject. It was the beginning of a long working relationship between Brady and Grant.

A Valuable Historical Record

Leaving Brady, Grant officially took command of the Union Army. The general was not the only one who felt obliged to get on with his war duties. Brady left the capital in early May 1864, planning to photograph more military campaigns and battlefields.

Among the more important of these photos from a historical standpoint are those Brady took in June 1864. He and an assistant camped with the members of a Union cannon battery near Petersburg, Virginia. The battery was under the command of Captain James Cooper. Cooper later recalled:

> *Our corps [of cannons] arrived in front of Petersburg on June 17, 1864. [We got] into position on the evening of that day and engaged the Confederate batteries . . . commanded by General Beauregard. . . . While occupying this position, Mr. Brady took the photographs [on June 21]. . . . In [one] photograph, you will notice a person in civilian clothes. This is Mr. Brady or his assistant, but I think it is Mr. Brady himself.*[16]

Brady did not take these photos during the actual battle. But all of the men and equipment involved in that battle were still in place when he arrived. So the

Brady took this shot while he was with a Union Army encampment at Petersburg, Virginia. Troops rest in the trenches while two officers check out the enemy's position.

pictures constitute a valuable historical record of the campaign. According to Frassanito:

> *Although [the photos] were probably not taken "under fire," they were nevertheless recorded under circumstances as close to actual combat as the state of the art permitted during the Civil War period. The immediacy is definitely there—and it is for this reason . . . that historians will be forever indebted to the efforts of [Brady and his colleagues].*[17]

7

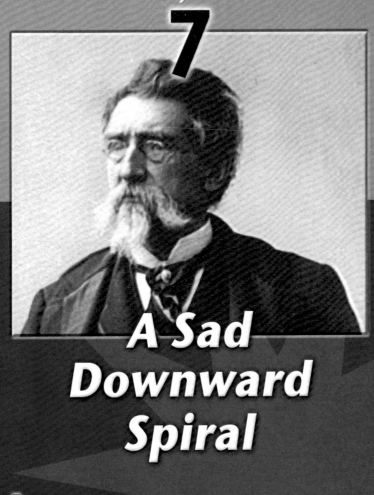

A Sad Downward Spiral

In the immediate aftermath of the Civil War, Mathew Brady continued to take photos of key national leaders and events. On April 20, 1865, for example, he photographed Robert E. Lee. This was only eleven days after Lee had surrendered his army. (The fighting continued in some areas until May 1865.)

Yet the high point of Brady's career had passed. As the months rolled by, a disturbing fact became increasingly clear. He was no longer the most popular and successful photographer in the capital. That honor now rested with Alexander Gardner. True, Brady still took all photos of General Grant in the field. But it was Gardner who took the last photos of Abraham Lincoln. He also obtained permission from federal authorities to photograph Lincoln's assassins.

One reason for this turn of events was the nature of the photography business itself. More and more talented individuals entered the field each year. And many of them were hard workers, innovators, or both. So competition among photographers was greater than ever. Also, money troubles had occupied much of Brady's career. At the end of the war he was nearly broke and badly in debt.

Capturing History

Despite these difficulties, in 1865 Brady was only about forty-two. He was still ambitious and energetic. Moreover, he considered himself the most distinguished photographer around.

The session with the leading Confederate general seemed to confirm that opinion. Certainly no other photographer was bold enough to approach Robert E. Lee so soon after his surrender. Brady thought it was worth a shot. So he went to Lee's house at 707 East Franklin Street in Richmond and knocked on the door. A servant answered and the visitor identified himself. Several seconds later, Lee stepped out onto the porch. Twenty years before, Lee, then a lieutenant colonel in

Brady was able to capture the funeral procession down Pennsylvania Avenue in Washington, D.C., for President Abraham Lincoln in 1865.

the U.S. Army, had posed for photos in Brady's New York gallery. But now the situation was quite different, Lee pointed out. "It is utterly impossible, Mr. Brady," he said. "How can I sit for a photograph with the eyes of the world upon me as they are today?"[1]

Brady did not accept Lee's polite refusal. The historical importance of recording the general's image at this moment seemed simply too great. So Brady spoke to both Lee's wife and Robert Ould, a judge and close

Brady chose Robert E. Lee's home as the setting for this photo of the Confederate general.

friend of both Lee's and Brady's. The photographer had met both of them before the war. He now urged them to try to change Lee's mind. They managed to do so. The next day Lee gave Brady an hour-long sitting outside the back door of the general's home.

Soon afterward, Brady took another important photo. On April 14, 1865, almost a week before Lee sat for Brady, President Lincoln had been assassinated. Later that spring, a publisher, James Bachelder, hired noted artist Alonzo Chappel. He asked Chappel to do a painting of Lincoln's deathbed scene. No photo had been taken of that historic scene. So Bachelder and Chappel hired Brady. All of the men who had been present when Lincoln died posed in Brady's studio. And Chappel used the photos as guides to produce his famous work *The Last Hours of Lincoln*.

A Crushing Disappointment

These photos that Brady took in the weeks and months following the end of the war turned out to have great historical value after his death. But their financial value to him at the time was minimal. For the past three years, business at his Washington gallery had been steadily declining.

Brady had tried to stop this downward trend in September 1864. He had sold a half-interest in the gallery to its manager, James Gibson. But the money Gibson had put up for the deal had paid Brady's bills for only a few months. Brady had also used up all the money in his savings. So by the summer of 1865, he and his wife were almost broke. They had to borrow money every month to support themselves and their galleries. In this way, they sank deeper and deeper into debt.

Once more, Brady attempted to turn his failing financial situation around. This time, he wanted to sell his war photos. He had always counted on them to make a fortune for him. Surely, he thought, the public would clamor to see a full or partial photographic record of the historic conflict.

But Brady was in for a crushing disappointment. The New York Historical Society agreed to let him show many of his war photos in its gallery. The press and critics praised the exhibition. Brady asked the historical society's directors to buy the photos for a large sum and put them on permanent display. At first, this idea seemed very appealing to many people. Several noted public figures offered their support. General Grant, for instance, wrote to Brady in February 1866:

> I am glad to learn that you have determined to place [your war photos] on permanent exhibition. . . . The collection will be valuable to the student and the artist of the present generation. But how much more valuable it will be to the future generations.[2]

The directors of the historical society also praised the photos and told Brady they would likely buy them.

The deal never went through, however. It became clear to all involved that a permanent exhibition of the photos would not be profitable. The fact was that many people had put the war behind them.

Increasingly Desperate

The loss of the historical society deal hit Brady hard. The Washington gallery closed and went bankrupt. It soon went up for sale at public auction. Desperate, Brady borrowed seventy-six hundred dollars, a huge sum at the time. With this money in hand, he attended the auction and bought back his gallery.

Brady turned to different strategies to pay his other debts. In 1869, he reluctantly sold some New York real estate he had bought years before. He also approached the U.S. Congress. He wanted the legislative body to buy all of his war photos. These would then become a major, permanent public record of the Civil War. Various politicians showed an interest in this project. But year after year they delayed voting to fund it.

Meanwhile, Brady's life continued its sad downward spiral. He went bankrupt again in January 1873, this time in New York. Brady knew that the court would seize all of his equipment. It would then sell the items to pay his debts. So at the last minute he used some political connections. The sheriff of New York City, the friend of a friend, put nineteen cartloads of Brady's equipment in storage. This was done before the bankruptcy court issued its seizure order. So the items were safe for the moment.

However, Brady still faced financial hard times. He lost his New York galleries, and he and his wife moved to Washington permanently. There, he transferred ownership of the Washington gallery to her. This attempt to keep creditors from seizing the studio worked for the time being. Later, ownership of the gallery passed to Julia's brother, Samuel Handy, and her nephew, Levin Handy.

A Temporary Turn for the Better

After these setbacks, Brady redoubled his efforts to persuade Congress to buy his photos. In a letter dated October 30, 1874, he tried to get the support of the secretary of war, William W. Belknap. "I have spent a lifetime in collecting the works I now offer," Brady said. "I have impoverished myself and broken up my business." Many government officials had encouraged him to go out and photograph the war, he recalled. "Yet I have never received a dollar" from the government in return. Brady concluded by saying that Congress's approval of the sale would be "common justice."[3]

Such pleas finally had the desired effect. The following year, Congress voted to buy Brady's photos for twenty-five thousand dollars. The collection contained 5,712 glass negatives. There were also numerous prints that had been made from the negatives.

Most of this windfall went instantly to pay Brady's debts. But he fortunately had enough left over to redecorate his gallery. His plan was to reestablish himself as the country's leading photographer. To that end, he invited many politicians and other famous people to a big party at the gallery. In the five years that followed, many

Thomas Edison (pictured in a photo by Brady) was the inventor who went on to create the incandescent light bulb and was an innovator in early film-making.

well-known individuals sat for him. He photographed the great inventor Thomas Edison. He also captured the likeness of Susan B. Anthony, the renowned crusader for women's right to vote. Other notables who came to Brady's studio in this period included Salmon P. Chase, chief justice of the Supreme Court; President Rutherford B. Hayes; and James A. Garfield, who would succeed Hayes as president in 1881.

One of the most memorable of these sittings was one with Samuel Langhorne Clemens. Better known as Mark Twain, he was the author of *The Adventures of Tom Sawyer* and *Huckleberry Finn.* At the time, Twain was in his forties. He posed with two friends. One of them was reporter George A. Townsend, Brady's friend. While at the gallery, Twain was extremely impressed by the array of photos on the wall. He said there was "a fortune" tied up in these pictures of famous people. "Brady," he added, "if I were not so tied up in my [own] enterprises, I would join you."[4]

Ill and Destitute

Despite the sittings with famous people, Brady's gallery made less and less money. Eventually, he and his wife could no longer afford to live in the first-class National Hotel. First, they moved to a cheaper hotel. Then they resided in a series of run-down boardinghouses. Finally, the couple was forced to live in the gallery itself.

Making matters worse, Julia Brady suffered increasingly from a heart condition. The ailment caused her to become bedridden. As for her husband, his own eyesight

Mark Twain (center) posed with his friends George A. Townsend (right) and David Gray.

got worse and worse. He began wearing glasses with heavy, blue-tinted lenses. And in time he had to supplement these with a magnifying glass to read the newspaper. Brady also developed painful arthritis. Most of the time he was unable to work, so Levin Handy ran the gallery for him.

But Handy's management of the gallery did not last long. In 1881, one of the employees sued Brady for unpaid salary. The court ordered

Levin Handy ran Brady's gallery for a while. This photo was taken by Mathew Brady some time after 1880.

that the gallery be closed and sold to pay the debt. So in November of that year, the last of Brady's once-profitable studios shut down permanently. Brady and his wife were now nearly destitute. But for a while, he managed to make enough money to buy food and medicine. Whenever possible, he worked in the studios of leading local photographers.

The biggest blow of all for Brady came in 1887. That year his wife died of her heart condition. Brady and her nephew, Levin Handy, laid her to rest in Washington's Congressional Cemetery. Thereafter, Brady became ill-tempered and drank heavily. Once a

American Indian Visitors

Among Mathew Brady's more interesting clients during his last fruitful years were several Ponca Indians. They lived in Nebraska and came with Major Howard, an agent of the U.S. Bureau of Indian Affairs, to Brady's Washington gallery in the fall of 1877.

The visitors were very intrigued by the photos of famous people hanging in the reception hall. They had heard of General Grant and other American leaders. But this marked the first time they had ever seen what they looked like.

When Brady began to set up a group photo of the Ponca, they became reluctant. It appeared that they were worried that the camera might harm them in some way. Major Howard explained that the camera was not a weapon. He and Brady showed them the lenses, glass plates, and other camera parts up close. Finally, the visitors agreed to sit for some group photos. However, they still refused to be photographed individually.

The Ponca Indians at first feared Brady's camera, but he finally got them to pose for a picture.

vital, pleasant person, he was now a miserable, cranky old man. He was also so poor that he had to move in with Levin Handy.

Return to New York

If Brady thought his life could not get any worse, he was wrong. One day in April 1895, he was crossing Fourteenth Street in the capital. He was then about seventy-two and walked slowly with the aid of a cane. Suddenly a horse-drawn carriage struck him. Bleeding and unconscious, he fell to the pavement. Afterward he spent time in the hospital. During the months that followed, Brady required crutches to get around.

Photographing the First Lady

In the last few years of his life, Brady occasionally took photographs at various locations in Washington. Usually his nephew, Levin Handy, helped him transport and set up the equipment. One of Brady's last noteworthy photos was taken on February 25, 1892. He was nearly seventy at that time.

The main subject of the picture was Caroline Harrison, wife of the then sitting president, Benjamin Harrison. It was a group shot. Caroline Harrison was the vice president of the Daughters of the American Revolution. (That famous women's group is dedicated to promoting historic preservation and patriotism. To be accepted as a member, a woman must prove that an ancestor took part in the American Revolution.) Brady posed her in a central position among several other members of the organization.

After the sitting, the first lady asked Brady to show her a picture of her husband taken decades before. Brady had photographed Benjamin Harrison in 1865. At the time Harrison was a Union Army general. Seeing the old photo, Caroline Harrison suggested that Brady should photograph her husband again. But that future sitting never happened.

This photo of Mathew Brady in 1889 was possibly taken by his nephew, Levin Handy.

It was more and more difficult for Levin Handy to care for his uncle. So in the summer of that year Brady accepted a kind offer. He was an honorary member of an army militia unit (having been given that honor many years before). The regular members of the unit—New York City's 7th Regiment Infantry—now heard about his plight. They rented a small apartment for him in that city. It was located at 126 East Tenth Street.

Brady's "brothers" in the 7th Regiment also decided to throw a large party in his honor. It was scheduled for late January 1896. A number of well-known people were invited. All would watch Brady show slides of his renowned war photos. But this gala event was not destined to take place. Fate was about to deal Mathew Brady his last losing hand.

8

Brady's Legacy: "The Eye of History"

Though he was aging and in pain, during the fall of 1895 Mathew Brady kept quite busy. He spent a good deal of time preparing for his upcoming party and photo exhibition in January. He was excited about the fact that people still held him in such high regard. Perhaps there might be more such exhibitions of his work in the months and years to come. In a letter, he told his nephew, Levin Handy, that he hoped one success might lead to others.

But suddenly Brady's enthusiasm was dimmed by a health crisis. In November 1895, he developed a painful kidney condition. A close friend, William Riley, took him to New York's Presbyterian Hospital. They had to go to the charity wing because Brady lacked the money to pay for his care. "He is very weak," Riley wrote to Levin Handy. "But I am in hopes that he will . . . gain strength. . . . I shall make a point to see him every day."[1]

Brady did seem to get better for a while. But soon after New Year's Day in 1896, he took a turn for the worse. His health continued to decline. And at 5 P.M. on January 15, he died in the hospital. In another letter to Handy, Riley described his friend's last few days: "Brady was conscious. But for two or three days he was unable to speak on account of the swelling in his throat. I don't think he realized he was dying."[2]

Soon after Brady's passing, Riley went to the deceased's apartment. There, he sorted through his friend's belongings. Then Riley wrote to Handy, saying that he had found few items of any particular value. The only clothes, Riley said, were some old shirts, underwear, and socks, along with two coats. He informed Handy that he would donate these to charity. There was also a very old and worthless watch and a ring. Long ago, the Prince of Wales had given the ring to Brady during a photographic session. Thinking it might have some sentimental value, Riley sent the item to Handy.

Riley also saw to it that Brady's body was transported to Washington, D.C. Levin Handy and his wife made the funeral arrangements. (The members of New York's 7th Regiment paid part of the funeral costs.) Brady was buried beside his wife in Washington's Congressional Cemetery. There, he rested among many other well-known Americans, such as Henry Clay, a senator, and John Quincy Adams, a president.

Correcting Brady's Headstone

In the decades following Mathew Brady's death, thousands of people saw his headstone in Washington's Congressional Cemetery. But few realized that the marker contained a serious error. It listed his death as 1895. Yet he had died in January 1896.

In 1988, a group of Civil War enthusiasts from Warren, Ohio, visited the cemetery. When they saw Brady's headstone, they immediately noticed the error. They felt that the mistake must be corrected to honor his memory. They paid for a new headstone, which correctly lists the date of his death as 1896. Brady's birth date is uncertain. So they listed it as CA (meaning *circa*, or "about") 1822. The caption on the stone now reads: "Mathew B. Brady, CA 1822–1896, renowned photographer of the Civil War."

Advancing the Art

Mathew Brady left behind a truly impressive legacy. First, he had significantly advanced the art of photography. He had also boosted the careers of many of the leading photographers of that century. Overall, as one of his modern biographers puts it, Brady was "the most important single force in the first generation of American photography."[3]

In addition, Brady created the first large-scale photographic record of a war. His thousands of Civil War pictures captured the conflict for his generation and future ones. Indeed, he possessed a strong sense of history. And he was one of the first people to recognize the potential of photography to preserve historical events. He was reported to have said: "The camera is the eye of history."[4]

The Handy Collection

The most tangible aspect of Brady's legacy was the enormous quantity of photos he left behind. At the time of his death, these were divided into several separate collections. One of the two principle ones belonged to Levin Handy. Brady and Handy had worked together a great deal in the older man's last decades. Handy inherited thousands of his uncle's negatives and prints. (Most of these were taken after the Civil War.)

Handy also ended up with Brady's remaining cameras and other photographic equipment. Using these, Handy opened his own studio in Washington. He swiftly became as famous in that town as his uncle had been. President Theodore Roosevelt and many other noted figures sat for Handy. The latter also photographed thousands of important government documents. (In 1903, the original Declaration of Independence and several other priceless documents almost burned in a fire. To help preserve them, the government hired Handy to photograph them.) It can be argued that Handy's distinguished career was a key part of Brady's legacy.

As for the Brady photos Handy owned, Handy guarded them closely for decades. When he died in 1932, his two daughters, Alice H. Cox and Mary H. Evans, inherited the pictures. In 1954, Cox and Evans agreed to sell the collection to the Library of Congress for twenty-five thousand dollars. There, the precious items were carefully cataloged and preserved.[5]

From left to right, Mary Evans, Alice Cox, and Edgar Cox look at prints from their relative, Mathew Brady, as they prepare to donate the items to the Library of Congress.

A Part of History

Another major collection of Brady's photos was the one he had given to Anthony & Company to satisfy his debts. These pictures changed hands several times in the late 1800s and early 1900s. Then, in 1907 Edward B. Eaton purchased them. Eaton published a leading historical journal, *Connecticut Magazine.* In the same year he acquired the photos, he gathered them into a large book. He titled it *Original Photographs Taken on the Battlefields During the Civil War by Mathew B. Brady and Alexander Gardner.*

Eaton died in 1942. His collection of Brady's photos passed to a publishing company in Springfield, Massachusetts. Two years later, officials at the Library of Congress bought the pictures from that company. Like those acquired from Handy later, they were sorted and preserved. The collection of Brady photos at the Library of Congress is now called the Brady-Handy Collection. Later, the National Portrait Gallery and National Archives bought other smaller collections of Brady's works.

The combined collection of Brady pictures in these three national institutions constitutes one of the nation's great treasures. Today, students, historians, journalists, and others can see and study them. The photos also continue to fascinate and educate new generations. In 1990, filmmaker Ken Burns first aired his acclaimed TV series *The Civil War.* He used many of Brady's photos in each episode. In fact, Burns claimed that he could not have made the series without them.

This photo of a girl named Teresa Cavens, taken in one of Brady's studios between 1855 and 1865, is one of the thousands that is now part of the Brady-Handy Collection at the Library of Congress.

There is no doubt that Brady would be greatly pleased by these developments. "My greatest aim," he once said, "has been to . . . make [photography] a great and truthful medium of history."[6] He definitely fulfilled this goal. In so doing, as he had hoped would happen, he became a part of history himself.

CHRONOLOGY

ca. 1822 — Mathew Brady is born in Warren County, in upstate New York.

ca. 1839 — At the age of about sixteen, travels to Saratoga Springs, New York, and meets painter William Page. Later that year, or perhaps early the following year, the two move to New York City.

1844 — Opens his first photographic gallery in New York City.

1845 — Photographs renowned former U.S. president Andrew Jackson.

ca. 1848 — Opens his first gallery in Washington, D.C.

1849 — Photographs presidents James K. Polk and Zachary Taylor and former first lady Dolley Madison.

ca. 1850 — Marries Juliette (Julia) Elizabeth Handy.

1851 — Travels to England to attend the Great Exhibition, the first world's fair, where he wins the top photography prize.

1853 — Opens his second New York gallery.

1856 — Hires Scottish photographer Alexander Gardner.

1858 — Opens his second Washington gallery (the first one having closed a few years before); puts Gardner in charge of the operation.

1859 — Opens his third New York gallery.

1860 — Photographs Abraham Lincoln for the first time.

1861 — The American Civil War begins. Brady tries to take pictures at the first battle of Bull Run; also photographs Lincoln again, along with members of Lincoln's family.

1862 — Sends two assistants to photograph the bloody battle of Antietam.

1864 — Photographs Lincoln again, as well as Ulysses S. Grant for the first time; also sells half ownership of the Washington gallery to his assistant, James Gibson.

1865 — The Civil War ends; Brady photographs Confederate general Robert E. Lee shortly after Lee's surrender; Lincoln is murdered.

1867 — Due to financial troubles, loses his Washington gallery; manages to buy it back at an auction.

1873 — Goes bankrupt in New York; soon loses New York galleries.

1875 — The U.S. Congress buys more than five thousand of his photos for twenty-five thousand dollars.

1887 — Julia Brady dies, leaving her husband grief-stricken.

1895 — Brady is struck by a horse-drawn carriage in Washington; recovers but must use crutches to get around.

1896 — Dies from a kidney ailment in New York's Presbyterian Hospital.

1944–
1954 — The U.S. Library of Congress buys the bulk of Brady's photos and catalogues and preserves them.

CHAPTER NOTES

CHAPTER 1
War Is No Picnic

1. James M. McPherson, *Battle Cry of Freedom: The Civil War Era* (New York: Oxford University Press, 2003), p. 341.
2. Bob Zeller, *The Blue and Gray in Black and White: A History in Civil War Photography* (London: Praeger, 2005), p. 57.
3. McPherson, p. 344.
4. Samuel S. Cox, *Three Decades of Federal Legislation, 1855–1885* (Providence, R.I.: R.A. Reid, 1885), p. 158.
5. William A. Frassanito, *Antietam: The Photographic Legacy of America's Bloodiest Day* (New York: Scribner's, 1982), p. 29.
6. Stephen G. Hyslop, *Eyewitness to the Civil War* (Washington, D.C.: National Geographic, 2006), p. 399.
7. George A. Townsend, "Still Taking Pictures," *The World*, April 12, 1891, p. 26.
8. Zeller, p. 60.
9. Ibid.
10. Frassanito, p. 54.

CHAPTER 2
A Young Man in the Big City

1. Dorothy M. Kunhardt and Philip B. Kunhardt, Jr., *Mathew Brady and His World* (Alexandria, Va.: Time-Life Books, 1977), p. 36.
2. "M. B. Brady: Phrenological Character and Biography," *American Phrenological Journal*, vol. 27, no. 5, May 1858, p. 66.
3. Kunhardt and Kunhardt, p. 39.

4. Ibid., p. 40.
5. Ibid., p. 39.
6. James D. Horan, *Mathew Brady: Historian With a Camera* (New York: Crown, 1980), p. 6.
7. Getty Museum, "John Plumbe, Jr." The Getty: Artists, n.d., <http://www.getty.edu/art/gettyguide/artMaker Details?maker=1979> (October 11, 2007).
8. Horan, p. 6.
9. Ibid.
10. Kunhardt and Kunhardt, p. 40.

CHAPTER 3
"Brady of Broadway"

1. Bob Zeller, *The Blue and Gray in Black and White: A History of Civil War Photography* (London: Praeger, 2005), pp. 15, 19.
2. Mary Panzer, *Mathew Brady and the Image of History* (Washington, D.C.: Smithsonian Institution, 1997), p. 42.
3. Roy Meredith. *Mathew Brady's Portrait of an Era* (New York: W.W. Norton, 1982), p. 30.
4. Ibid., p. 29.
5. Zeller, p. 110.
6. Dorothy M. Kunhardt and Philip B. Kunhardt, Jr., *Mathew Brady and His World* (Alexandria, Va.: Time-Life Books, 1977), p. 43.
7. Meredith, p. 35.
8. T. B. Thorpe, "Webster, Clay, Calhoun, and Jackson: How They Sat for Their Daguerreotypes," *Harper's New Monthly Magazine*, vol. 38, no. 228, May 1869, p. 789.
9. Kunhardt and Kunhardt, p. 45.

CHAPTER 4
At the Height of Success

1. Roy Meredith, *Mathew Brady's Portrait of an Era* (New York: W.W. Norton, 1982), p. 50.

2. George A. Townsend, "Still Taking Pictures," *The World*, April 12, 1891, p. 26.

3. Meredith, p. 49.

4. Roger Butterfield, "The Camera Comes to the White House," *American Heritage*, 2006, <http://www.american heritage.com/articles/magazine/ah/1964/5/1964_5_33. shtml> (October 12, 2007).

5. James D. Horan. *Mathew Brady: Historian With a Camera* (New York: Crown, 1980), p. 11.

6. Townsend, p. 26.

7. Ibid.

8. Horan, p. 6.

9. Ibid., p. 14.

10. Dorothy M. Kunhardt and Philip B. Kunhardt, Jr., *Mathew Brady and His World* (Alexandria, Va.: Time-Life Books, 1977), p. 48.

11. Townsend, p. 26.

12. Kunhardt and Kunhardt, p. 49.

CHAPTER 5
Photographing Lincoln

1. Dorothy M. Kunhardt and Philip B. Kunhardt, Jr., *Mathew Brady and His World* (Alexandria, Va.: Time-Life Books, 1977), p. 90.

2. Harold Holzer, *Lincoln at Cooper Union* (New York: Simon and Schuster, 2004), p. 5.

3. Roy Meredith, *Mr. Lincoln's Camera Man: Mathew B. Brady* (New York: Dover, 1974), p. 67.

4. Paul White, "Mathew Brady," *Dickinson College—War and Remembrance,* 1998, <http://users.dickinson.edu/~osborne/ 404_98/whitep.htm> (October 12, 2007).

5. James D. Horan, *Mathew Brady: Historian With a Camera* (New York: Crown, 1980), p. 35.

6. Roy Meredith, *Mathew Brady's Portrait of an Era* (New York: W.W. Norton, 1982), p. 100.

7. Horan, p. 32.

8. "Autobiography of Andrew Dickinson White," *FullBooks. com*, n.d., <http://www.fullbooks.com/Autobiography-of-Andrew-Dickson-White3.html> (October 12, 2007).

9. Unpublished comments about Mathew Brady by Bob Zeller, February 27, 2007.

10. "Thomas D. Lincoln (1853–1871)," *Mr. Lincoln's White House*, 2007, <http://www.mrlincolnswhitehouse.org/inside.asp?ID=17&subjectID=2> (October 12, 2007).

CHAPTER 6
In the Heat of War

1. Marcus A. Root, *The Camera and Pencil* (New York: D. Appleton, 1864), p. 375.

2. Bob Zeller, *The Blue and Gray in Black and White: A History of Civil War Photography* (London: Praeger, 2005), p. 75.

3. Stephen G. Hyslop, *Eyewitness to the Civil War* (Washington, D.C.: National Geographic, 2006), pp. 164, 399.

4. William A. Frassanito, *Antietam: The Photographic Legacy of America's Bloodiest Day* (New York: Scribner's, 1982), pp. 15–16.

5. Zeller, p. 73.

6. Frassanito, pp. 53–54.

7. Ibid., p. 54.

8. Ibid.

9. Hyslop, p. 399.

10. Zeller, p. 104.

11. Ibid.

12. William A. Frassanito, *Gettysburg: A Journey in Time* (New York: Scribner's, 1975), p. 39.

13. Zeller, p. 104.

14. Roy Meredith, *Mathew Brady's Portrait of an Era* (New York: W.W. Norton, 1982), p. 136.

15. "Erasing Grant and/or Sherman," *War Historian.org*, 2005, <http://warhistorian.org/blog1/index.php?d=12&m=02&y=06&category=2> (October 14, 2007).

16. William A. Frassanito, *Grant and Lee: The Virginia Campaigns, 1864–1865* (New York: Scribner's, 1983), pp. 242, 245.
17. Ibid., p. 247.

CHAPTER 7
A Sad Downward Spiral

1. James D. Horan, *Mathew Brady: Historian With a Camera* (New York: Crown, 1980), p. 59.
2. Ibid., p. 73.
3. Mary Panzer, *Mathew Brady and the Image of History* (Washington, D.C.: Smithsonian Institution, 1997), p. 192.
4. George A. Townsend, "Still Taking Pictures," *The World*, April 12, 1891, p. 26.

CHAPTER 8
Brady's Legacy: "The Eye of History"

1. Roy Meredith, *Mr. Lincoln's Camera Man: Mathew B. Brady* (New York: Dover, 1974), p. 256.
2. Ibid., p. 258.
3. Dorothy M. Kunhardt and Philip B. Kunhardt, Jr., *Mathew Brady and His World* (Alexandria, Va.: Time-Life Books, 1977), p. 65.
4. James D. Horan, *Mathew Brady: Historian With a Camera* (New York: Crown, 1980), p. 90.
5. Today, the collection is available online. See "Brady-Handy Collection," *Library of Congress*, 2004, <http://www.loc.gov/rr/print/coll/222_bradyhandy.html> (October 14, 2007).
6. Mary Panzer, *Mathew Brady and the Image of History* (Washington, D.C.: Smithsonian Institution, 1997), p. 205.

GLOSSARY

anxiety—Extreme nervousness or worry.

arthritis—A painful condition affecting the elbows, knees, and other joints.

assassination—The murder of a prominent person.

bankruptcy—An official declaration that one does not have enough money to pay one's debts.

cabinet—The heads of the various departments of a democratic government.

camera obscura—In the early years of photography, a darkened room with a single hole through which light entered. The light projected an image of an outside scene onto one wall of the room.

competition—People, companies, or stores that vie with one another for business.

creditor—A person who loans someone money and expects to be paid back.

daguerreotype—In the early years of photography, a copper plate coated in silver. Light burned an image onto the plate.

destitute—Very poor and barely able to support oneself.

distinguished—Noteworthy, memorable, or famous.

engraving—A sketch or photo carved or transferred onto wood, metal, or paper.

exposure—In photography, when light enters the camera and records an image on a chemically treated plate or sheet of film.

federal—Relating to the national government.

inauguration—The official ceremony in which public figures take office.

president-elect—In a democracy, the title given to a newly elected president before he or she officially takes the oath of office.

recollections—Memories.

secede—To break away or separate from something, as in a state seceding from the Union.

wet-plate process—In the early years of photography, making photos on glass plates coated with chemicals.

FURTHER READING

Armstrong, Jennifer. *Photo by Brady: A Picture of the Civil War.* New York: Atheneum Books for Young Readers, 2005.

Bankston, John. *Louis Daguerre and the Story of the Daguerreotype.* Hockessin, Del.: Mitchell Lane Publishers, 2005.

Davis, William C. *The Civil War in Photographs.* London: Carlton, 2002.

Donlan, Leni. *Mathew Brady.* Chicago: Raintree, 2008.

Golay, Michael. *Civil War.* New York: Facts On File, 2003.

Pelusey, Michael and Jane. *Photography.* Philadelphia: Chelsea House, 2005.

Phillips, E. B. *Abraham Lincoln: From Pioneer to President.* New York: Sterling Pub. Co., 2007.

Sandler, Martin W. *America Through the Lens: Photographers Who Changed the Nation.* New York: Henry and Holt Co., 2005.

INTERNET ADDRESSES

The Civil War as Photographed by Mathew Brady
<http://www.archives.gov/education/lessons/
brady-photos/>

Mathew Brady's Portraits
<http://www.npg.si.edu/exh/brady/index.htm>

Selected Civil War Photographs
<http://memory.loc.gov/ammem/cwphtml/cw
phome.html>

INDEX